YOUR GUIDE T(

Google

Web Search

Your Guide to Google Web Search

How to Find the Information You Need on the Internet

by René Djurup

ISBN 13: 978-87-7793-029-4
ISBN 10:   87-7793-029-0

Trademarks
All terms in the book, for which Rebidu ApS was aware of a trademark claim, have been printed as suggested by the owner of the trademark. Rebidu ApS cannot warrant the accuracy of this information. Terms and names in the book are used for editorial purposes only with no intention of infringement of any trademark.

Disclaimer
Every precaution has been taken to ensure that the information in the book is accurate at the time of release for printing, but the author and publisher shall have no responsibility for any errors. The information in the book is provided on an "as is" basis. Neither the author nor the publisher shall have any liability to any person or entity with respect to any loss or damage caused by or allegedly caused by information contained in the book or by use hereof by any means.

Permissions and acknowledgement
The labeling of the screenshots of Google search pages, search results pages, etc. is by permission of Google, Inc.
The illustration on the cover is reproduced under a Standard License Agreement with iStockphoto. The illustration is made by the artist geopaul.

Contact
To report any error in the book, please send an e-mail to websearch@rebidu.com

YOUR GUIDE TO

Google
Web Search

How to Find the Information You Need on the Internet

René Djurup

Rebidu ApS, 2010

Chapter 3
Using Advanced Search   107

Chapter 4
Using Operators   143

Appendix A

Introduction

Today, close to two billion people have access to the Internet and use the World Wide Web (also known as the Web) to find the information they need. The Web contains billion of documents and is the most important information source for people in the developed countries. In most countries, people can publish what they want on the Web. The number of Web pages is growing day after day at an ever-increasing speed. There is no system for reviewing or organizing the enormous amount of diverse information floating around on the Web.

The vast and rapidly growing amount of Web documents often makes it difficult to find what you need. Instead of getting pages with the concrete information you are looking for, you frequently get lots of pages that are irrelevant to your topic. You may regularly find thousands of pages, but no or only a few real hits. This happens even when there actually are many relevant pages on the Web.

The good news is that the information you need almost always exists on the Web, and that it can be found by use of the free program Google Web Search - commonly just called Google.

Google Web Search has all the features and tools needed to make highly effective Web searches that deliver the results you need. To succeed, you must, however, know how the Google search engine really works, how the Google search tools work, and when and how to use the various tools.

Google Web Search is so good at finding simple, concrete information (the location of the nearest pizza shop, flight schedules, and so on) that you may easily be misled to believe that Google automatically finds all types of information for you. This is unfortunately not the case. For more demanding tasks, such as finding reliable health guidance, you often need considerable Web search skills. Google Web Search can help you to find such information, but here you need to take control over the search process and to use some of the more advanced features and tools.

To benefit from the Google Web Search features and tools, you obviously need to know that they exist, how they work, and when to use them. Several studies suggest that most people only use a fraction of the power of Google Web Search. As an example, most users just enter one or two keywords in the Google search box when they want to find information. They seldom write queries with three or more keywords nor do they use any of the advanced search features. If you are using Google Web Search the same way as most other people do, you can benefit greatly from learning better search techniques. Effective Web search is not an art, but a simple craft that can be learned by everyone in a short time. In this book, you can learn the techniques needed to become a highly skilled Web searcher.

My aim with the book is to give you a reliable, comprehensive, and up-to-date guide to Google Web Search. Below, I'll explain in more details, what I mean by reliable, comprehensive, and up-to-date.

The book gives you reliable guidance in the sense that the techniques described have been tested in real search situations. For each technique, I have in small experiments tried to assess, if it increases the number of relevant results on the top of the results list. Most of the examples have been tested several times over time to see, if the findings are consistent.

The book is comprehensive in the sense that it tries to cover all the important aspects of Google Web Search. Each feature is discussed in details. The book focuses on search for information in text form. Other types of Web search, for example, for images, is only very sparsely described or not described at all. Features, which require that you have a Google account, are not discussed.

The book is fully up-to-date. It covers all Google Web Search features introduced until the end of March 2010. All guidance is based on how Google Web Search works today. Some advices may, therefore, deviate from what you find in other, older books, and in documents on the Web.

Google says in their official blog (Jan. 22, 2010): *"The Google that you used today is actually better than the Google that you used yesterday. On a daily basis, we make a number of algorithmic enhancements and release other search features that ultimately make finding what you're looking for quick, easy and enjoyable"*.

Google's statement illustrates how challenging it is to write an up-to-date book about Google Web Search.

To assure that you have the most current information about Google Web Search available, the book has been continuously updated until the release for print. Furthermore, most of the search techniques you learn are general methods that will be valid, even if Google should decide to modify the search page or some other part of Google Web Search. In addition, the book will be supported by its own Web site to assist you in keeping your Google Web Search knowledge and capabilities current. You'll find the Web site on the address:

www.YourWebSearchGuide.com

On this site, you'll find any important updates to the book, corrections, and additional material related to Google Web Search. The Web site will be launched end of April 2010.

You won't find any references in the book. Most books about Internet search in general and about Google Web Search in particular quickly become outdated. Instead of listing some good, but partly outdated books, I plan to review some interesting books on the book's Web site www.YourWebSearchGuide.com. Here you'll also find a number of interesting links to Web pages dealing with Google Web Search and general aspects of Internet search.

A few practical comments:

You don't need to have any previous knowledge about Google Web Search to benefit from the book. The book is written with international readers in mind. The idea is that it should be easy to read for people who don't have English as first language. Readability has been prioritized higher than elegance. I hope readers with English as first language will bear with me for the plain English.

Most people use one of the newer versions of Microsoft Internet Explorer when they surf the Web. For this reason, I have chosen to use Internet Explorer 8 for all screenshots shown in the book. You can use all the techniques and tools discussed with any modern Web browser (Chrome, Firefox, Internet Explorer, Opera, Safari, and so on).

None of the techniques and tools described requires that you establish a Google account and sign in before you search.

The book contains numerous screenshots to illustrate the search techniques and tools described. When complex Google Web Search elements, for example, the results page, are described, you are first shown a figure displaying the element in its entirety. The idea is to give you an overview of the element, for instance, the results page. In the subsequent description of the figure, details of the figure are displayed in close relation to the text to make it easier for you to follow the description. Furthermore, each part of a complex figure is as a rule labeled with a circled letter to make reference to the details easier.

You'll find numerous cross-references in the book. For cross-references to figures not occurring on the page you are reading, you get both the figure number and the page number where the figure occurs. On a given page, the page number for a figure occurring on another page is only shown for the first cross-reference.

Keywords and other things you have to enter in a search box are in the body text typed with italics (as in *keyword*). In captions to figures, which are themselves typed with italics, keywords are shown in regular types (as in keyword).

When you have to click on a button or to press a key on the keyboard, the button or key is shown in bold (as in Press **Enter**).

Google trademarks and terms are typed, spelled, and shown as Google uses them.

Last, but not least, I just want to say that it has been a pleasure to write the book. I learned a lot during the process. I hope you'll enjoy reading the book as much as I enjoyed writing it – and that you'll learn at least as much as I did.

René Djurup

April 2010

Chapter 1

Google Search Essentials

Before we begin, we should establish a common starting point. To this end, we need to look at the same Google search page in the same language.

If you live in US and have the US Google homepage (www.google.com) in English as your homepage, you are ready to go.

If you live outside the US, you should start by loading the Google US homepage and setting the language to English. You can read in the next section how to do this.

Loading the US Google Homepage

First, try to load the US Google search page by entering www.google.com in your Web browser's address bar (Figure 1-1).

Figure 1-1   Enter www.google.com to go to the Google US homepage

If you live outside the US, Google will usually redirect you to your local Google homepage (Figure 1-2, page 6). There are currently (February 2010) 179 local Google homepages. If your country doesn't yet have a local Google homepage, you'll remain on the US Google homepage.

If you have been redirected to your local homepage, Google displays the name of your country just below the Google logo (Figure 1-2, A). To go to the US Google homepage, click *Google.com in English* (Figure 1-2, B).

Google remembers this setting. Next time you try to load the US homepage you are usually not taken back to your local homepage, but to the US search page, as you want. However, this requires that your browser is set to accept cookies - and that the cookies are not deleted, when you close your browser. You can read more about this on page 182.

Figure 1-2   The local Danish Google homepage

When you click *Google.com in English*, Google also changes the language to English. You should now be looking at the US homepage in English (Figure 1-3).

Figure 1-3   The US Google homepage in English

Google still knows where you and your PC are located. Google knows this from your IP address. If you live outside the US, the US Google homepage gives you an option to go back to your local homepage at any time. You simply click *Go to Google Country* (Figure 1-3, D), where *Coun-*

6

try is the name of your country. In Figure 1-3, D (page 6) it is *Danmark*. Note that Google uses the local spelling (Danmark) – not the US spelling (Denmark).

Figure 1-4   Alternative US Google search homepage (Nov. 18, 2009)

Note about Search Settings (Global Preferences)

In this chapter, I presume that you haven't changed the Search settings - also known as Global preferences - with the possible exception of the interface language. The interface language is the language Google uses for menu texts, messages, hints, and so on (see also page 173). You can read about the Search settings (Global preferences) in Appendix A (starting on page 171).

For each setting listed below, you find more information on the page number stated in parentheses. For now, your Search settings (Global preferences) should be:

- Interface language: English (page 173)
- Search language: English (page 175)
- Safe Surf Filtering: Use moderate filtering (page 179)
- Number of Results: Display 10 results per page (page 180)
- Results Window: Leave the check box open (page 181)
- Query Suggestion: Provide query suggestions in the search box (page 181)

The US Google Web Search Page

The Google search homepage is very simple to use. Just enter one or more words (for example *google web search*) into the search box (Figure 1-3, A, page 6) and click the button **Google Search** (Figure 1-3, B). Google then displays a number of search results pages. As standard, each page displays 10 results.

Google displays at most 1,000 results (100 pages of 10 results each in the standard setting) for a search (see page 27). The results are ranked. The ones Google thinks are most relevant to your search are displayed first (see page 29).

Google displays the results on so-called search results pages. In this book, I usually just call them results pages. You can see an example on a results page in Figure 1-5. You are not meant to be able to read the text or study the details in Figure 1-5. We go through the results page in significant details in Chapter 2.

Don't use the I'm Feeling Lucky button
You shouldn't use the I'm Feeling Lucky button. When you click this button, Google only displays the top result. You almost always benefit from seeing a list of results.

Some Important Definitions and Concepts

Before we move on, we define some important concepts in relation to Web search. They are listed in the order, in which you probably will meet them, when you start searching.

Figure 1-5   A results page for the search google web search

Keyword

Any word you enter in the Google search box (Figure 1-3, A, page 6) is a keyword. In this book, keywords are typed with italics (as in *italics*) in the body text. In captions to the figures, keywords are typed with regular types, as the captions are typed with italics (see example in Figure 1-5 above). Keywords are typed with lowercase letters. This also applies for proper names such as *google*. It doesn't matter whether you use lowercase or uppercase letters.

Exact phrase

An exact phase is a sequence of keywords. If you want to search for an exact phrase, enclose the exact phrase within quotation marks (as in *"google web search"*). You should only search for "meaningful" sequences of keywords.

9

Search

The search is the process of finding Web documents that best possible match the keywords or the exact phrase. Search is often used as a synonym for query (see below).

Query

A query is the keywords and any exact phrase describing the information you ask the search engine to find in the Google databases. In other words, the query is all the keywords you enter into the search box. The term query is often used as a synonym for search. In this book, the term query is used the narrow sense as defined here.

Google

Google is a trademark of Google Inc. and is strictly speaking the name of the company Google Inc. However, it has become practice to use Google as synonym for Google Web Search (see below). We follow this practice here, unless the use of the term Google Web Search is needed for clarity.

Google search

Google search is often used as a synonym for Google Web Search (see below).

Google Web Search

Google Web Search is the program, which Google uses to find the Web pages that best match your query, and to display the results ranked after importance (popularity) and relevance to your topic. Actually, it is not a single program, but several programs and computer techniques. All the search features and tools you can read about in the book are part of Google Web Search.

Results page

The results page is the page showing the Google search results (Figure 1-5). You can read about the results page in Chapter 2.

Google search engine

The term Google search engine is often used about the programs, which Google Web Search uses for finding pages with information matching your query. There is no exact definition of this term. In this book, Google search engine is used in a broad sense. It covers the Google programs at your PC, the programs at Google's servers, and other programs, which in some way are involved in responding to your query, finding and ranking the results, and displaying them.

Search engine

In this book, the term search engine (singular) is used with the same meaning as Google search engine. The term search engines (plural), in contrast, refers to search engines in general.

How to Use the Google Search Box

In this section, you are introduced to the very basics of a simple Google search. We get back to all the details later.

You start a search from the Google search box on the Google homepage. To start a search, just enter your keywords in the search box (Figure 1-6, A). Click the button **Google Search** (Figure 1-6, B) or press **Enter**.

Figure 1-6   The Google Search box on the US Google homepage

Google then finds and displays the Web pages, which best matches your keywords – and which are most popular (see page 29 for more information).

How to Write a Query

To find results of relevance to your topic you must first write a specific query. We'll discuss in details later how to best do this, but basically it takes two things to write a specific query. First, you should try to use words and word sequences that resemble those used by people writing about your topic on the Web. This may not be easy if you are completely new to a topic, but below (and later in this chapter) you get some suggestions how to do this. As you start learning about your topic, it becomes much easier to find the best search words. Second, you should use one or more of the many filters to reduce the amount of irrelevant results. We'll discuss the filters in details here and in later chapters.

Use Appropriate Words and Word Sequences

When people publish something on the Web, they generally write the text in "natural language", using words that are appropriate for the purpose. Among other things, this means:

- They use many words to describe the topic.

- They write the words in meaningful sequences - not as isolated keywords.

- They use everyday words when writing about everyday topics and technical words when writing about technical topics for peers.

In contrast, most people searching for information on the Web write very simple queries, often consisting of only one or two keywords (see also page 35). For popular topics, Google Web Search regularly finds relevant results, even when you use such simple queries. However, to find information about topics that are less popular, or that are difficult to describe appropriately by a simple query, you may need to write queries that are more powerful.

The important thing to notice here is that the more your query matches the text published on the Web, the better your chance is to find the information you want.

To improve the match between your query and the information on the Web, you should follow the general guidelines listed below:

- Use appropriate words (everyday words or technical words). As an example, you get different search results for the two queries *platelet disorders* and *thrombocytopathia*, although both terms, by and large, cover the same concept.

- Include all essential keywords - not only the words you think are the most important. It is important to describe your information need as completely as possible. See example below.

- Write the keywords as short meaning full sequences of words - not as isolated words in random order.

- If some words must occur in a specific order, try to enclose them within quotation marks.

- If you are looking for an answer to a specific question, it often helps to start with a common question phrase such as *How* to or *How do I* (see example below).

Example: Writing a complete query with appropriate words

As an example on some of the advices given above, let us assume that you live outside the US, own a company, and want to sell something in the US from a US distributor. You have heard that you may need a US Taxpayer Identification Number, also known as a TIN number. You want to know, if you need it, and if so, how to get it.

You start by entering *tin number* as your first query. You get 48.6 million search results. Among the top 10 results, you find general information about a TIN number, but no direct link to the form you need to fill in. However, you may find it, if you carefully read through the results on the first results page and follow some links - which may be time-consuming.

By adding the keyword *foreign* so the query becomes *tin number foreign*, you come down to 6.7 million results and get information that is more relevant to foreign individuals and companies. The first 10 results still don't give you a direct link to the form you need.

By adding the term *company*, you come down to 791,000 results, and you find the direct link to the form (SS-4) you need as the second result on the list. This illustrates the importance of including all keywords that describe your information need. It just took four appropriate keywords to get the job done.

This actually completes the task. However, in this example, a better initial query would have been *how to get a tin number as a foreign employer*. This query gives you only 40,000 results, and the form you need is shown under the first result (as an indented result, see page 81).

You could do even better as regards the number of results. By specifying that you want to search for the exact phrases *"tin number"* and *"foreign employer"*, so the query becomes *how to get a "tin number" as a "foreign employer"*, you come down to only 10 results, of which number two is the relevant one. You can read about the use of quotation marks to find exact phrases on page 39.

Finally, you could consider restricting the search the .gov domain (see page 121). By restricting the search to the domain .gov by adding *site:.gov* to the query so it becomes *how to get a "tin number" as a "foreign employer" site.gov*, you get down to one result plus one indented result, which contains the SS-4 form. You'll learn about the *site* operator later (see page 158).

The example shows how you by simple means can reduce the number of search results from more than 48 millions to only two results, of which one is the form you need.

In the section Use Natural Language to Get Relevant Results on page 17, you can read more about how to use natural language to get relevant results to the top of the results list.

When you try to write your queries as natural sentences, the tool Google Suggest usually comes up with useful proposals for how to continue (see details on page 18 to 22). This tells you which words and sentences other people are using. From Google's proposals, you get an idea about if you are on the right way, or if you need to modify your query already at this step. If you are completely new to a topic, you may not land at the most relevant results in the first hit, but you'll most likely get a good idea about which words to use in your next, refined search.

Use Filters to Restrict Your Search

Google is no doubt aware that most Web searches result in far too many results of low or no relevance. Google Web Search, therefore, comes with a number of tools, which you can use to reduce the total number of results and to increase the relevance of the results. These tools are generally called filters, because they filter out the irrelevant results and isolate the results of relevance to your search. By use of filters, you can, among other things, exclude unwanted words, restrict your search to a specific language, a specific filetype, or a certain period of time.

In this chapter, we focus on how to write specific queries. In later chapters, you'll learn methods for fine-tuning your search by using filters and other tools.

Know What You Can Search For

You can search for individual characters (such as *g* or *3*), one or more words (such as *google* or *google search*), and phrases, for example, *google search engine* (with or without quotation marks). With few exceptions, for example the symbol &, you can't search for symbols such as # or %. Some symbols have a special function in Google Web Search, for example, + (page 144), - (page 145), ~ (page 48), and * (page 49).

A phrase is a group of words that function as a single unit in a sentence. In search language, a phrase is often called an exact phrase – to stress that the words must occur in the order written. If you want to specify that the words must occur exactly as you enter them, you must enclose the phrase within quotation marks as in *"google search engine"*.

Use of exact phrases – small pieces of text as they occur in natural language – is often an effective way to find relevant results. Google by itself gives high priority to documents where the keywords occur in the order you type them – and close to each other. However, now and then you may benefit from telling Google explicitly that the words must occur exactly as written by using quotation marks. You can read about the use of exact phrases on page 39.

Start by Getting an Overview of Your Topic

When you start searching for information about a new topic, you first need to get an overview of it. To get an overview, just type a few keywords that describe the topic well. This sounds very simple and usually also is. However, it may take a little thinking - and sometimes experimentation - to find the keywords that best describe the topic. The tool Google Suggest, also known as Google Query suggestions, here often give you valuable clues (see Figure 1-7, page 16).

Let us as an example assume that you want to know more about *climate change*, *CO2*, and *greenhouse effect*. Here, *climate*, *CO2*, and *greenhouse* may be seen as the three primary keywords. When you enter a query containing all three of them, you get highly relevant results on the first results page.

By shuffling the keywords around, you'll find that the order doesn't matter. You get relevant results on the first results page with any combination. This shows that Google is very good at finding relevant results when you search for highly popular topics. You don't need to think much about how to write an effective query in this situation. Google does the job and its ranking system (page 29) works as intended. It displays the most relevant results on the top of the results page.

Note that even in this example, in which Google does an excellent job, you may benefit from using natural language (see below) and looking at Query suggestions. In everyday language, people often talk about the *effect of CO2* on the climate. As soon as you type *effect of co2*, Google suggests three relevant search terms (Figure 1-7). You learn that besides *climate*, which we already knew, *global warming* and *environment* are also popular search terms.

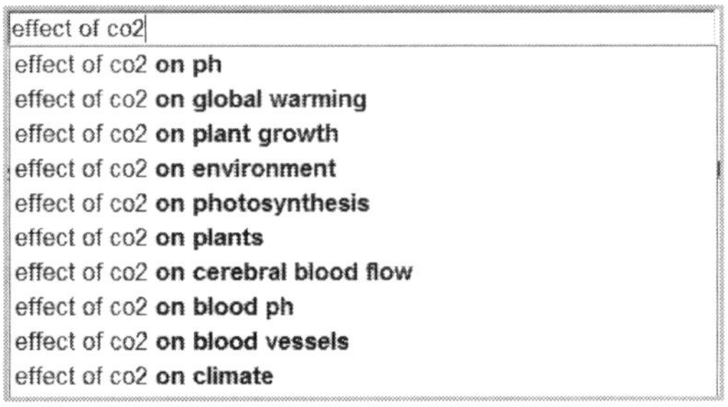

```
effect of co2|
effect of co2 on ph
effect of co2 on global warming
effect of co2 on plant growth
effect of co2 on environment
effect of co2 on photosynthesis
effect of co2 on plants
effect of co2 on cerebral blood flow
effect of co2 on blood ph
effect of co2 on blood vessels
effect of co2 on climate
```

Figure 1-7   Google suggests 10 popular queries

Write More Specific Queries When Needed

In many situations, the common search practice described above will not get you the relevant results you need. This often happens, when your topic is not particularly popular among the Web surfers in general. For such queries, you may find many popular pages, which are irrelevant to your search. I'll try to explain this in more details below.

Each page on the Web has a popularity score (page 31). This may go up or down over time, but it doesn't depend on your query. Whatever you search for, the popularity score for a page remains the same – at least within a shorter period. You can read more about the popularity score on page 31.

In contrast, the content score (page 31) for a page depends on your query. The closer your query matches the content on a page, the higher content score the page gets. If you write a simple query, consisting of only a couple of general keywords, a lot of pages on the Web will match your query. However, most likely, none of them is going to get a high content score, as the match between your query and the document text will be rather loose. This was illustrated in the example on page 13. You can read more about the content score on page 31.

To find pages with a low popularity score you need to increase the content score for the pages about your topic, so they get a high overall rank (see page 30), even when they have a low popularity score. You can do this by writing queries that closely match the content on the pages you are looking for. There is no general method for how to do this. However, the simple guidelines given below will take you a long way.

Use Natural Language to Get Relevant Results

As you have already seen in the example on page 13, your query must match the text found on the Web pages of relevance to your topic as much as possible. The closer you query resembles the text on a Web page, the better your chance to find the page. If you don't find the information you need after an initial simple query as described above, you may benefit from following the advices below. They repeat and expand the advices given earlier in this chapter.

- Try to write your query, so it resembles the text found on the Web pages of interest.
    - o Use words that match the content on the Web pages you want to find.
    - o Use simple, common words, if you are looking for information about everyday things and events.
    - o Use words used by professionals and experts, if you are looking for technical information.
- Write queries that describe your topics as completely as possible.
    - o Write queries consisting of minimum four keywords.
    - o Prefer even longer queries. The upper limit in Google Web Search is 32 keywords in one query.
    - o Enter the keywords in the sequence, in which they occur in the way we speak and write.
    - o Use quotation marks, if two or more words must occur in a specific order (as a word sequence).
- Use natural questions starting with *How to, How do I,* and so on to ask Google specific questions.
- Look at Google's query suggestions to get inspiration for relevant queries.
- Don't be afraid of using small common words – often known as stopwords (*a, the, I, you, is, are, above,* and so on). They don't stop anything, but often help finding citations, and so on, see below.

The use of most of the advices given above has already been illustrated in the example on page 13. In Figure 1-8 below, you find an example on the use of stopwords. As you can see, Google easily finds the famous phrase *to be or not to be* - even though it consists of stopwords only.

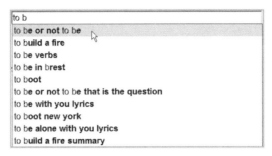

Figure 1-8   Google easily finds popular phrases

Contrary to the popular belief, Google often includes stopwords in the search - if they appear to be meaningful as for example in quotations, lyrics, proverbs, and so on.

Use Precise and Distinctive Words

Most often, the same thing or concept may be described with different words. Some words are more specific than others and help distinguish one thing from another. The more precisely you describe you topic, the better your chance is to find what you need. There is no general method to find the most precise words. The more your search and the more you know about a topic, the easier it will be. In the beginning, an up-to-date English dictionary and thesaurus will be a great help. Google's query suggestions may also be highly valuable. It suggests the terms, which are most popular. Even though you may prefer to write your query yourself, you may benefit from using query suggestions to give you a good idea about the terms used by others.

Google Suggest

As soon as you start typing, you'll see a box with 10 words and phrases below the search box (Figure 1-9, page 19). The 10 words are Google's suggestions for queries that you can make. The suggestions are based on what you have typed and what people in general are currently searching for. Be aware that Google suggests the 10 most popular current search terms. These are not necessarily the most relevant to your information need.

Google Query suggestions and Google Suggest
The tool, which Google today calls Google Suggest, was to begin with called Google Query suggestions or just Query suggestions. We here in general use the term Google Suggest for the tool itself, and the term query suggestions for the concrete query suggestions you get.

In the example below, you are going to see Google Suggest in operation.

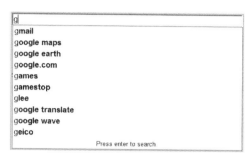

Figure 1-9   Google's suggestions for queries starting with g

Example: Searching Using Google Suggest
Let us start with a simple example. Imagine we want to know more about *google search engine* - the program Google uses to handle your queries. Start by entering *google*. Already when you start typing the first letter *g*, Google comes up with the 10 first suggestions (Figure 1-9).

Figure 1-10   The suggestions change as you type

When you type more letters, Google offers new suggestions. When you have typed *google se*, Google suggests *google search engine* (Figure 1-10). You can now jump to your search term *google search engine*. You don't have to finish typing the whole query. Just click on the query you want Google to carry out.

Google Suggest Pros and Cons

I find the Query suggestion feature to be one of the most useful Google search tools. Some people dislike Google Suggest – among other things because it may distract you from writing your "own" query (see page 22). I think the benefits by far outweigh any minor drawbacks.

Google Suggest Advantages

According to Google, you may benefit from Google Suggest in following ways:

- You may save typing. Often, Google suggests your search term before you have typed the full query (as in Figure 1-10, page 19).
- You may get suggestions for alternative spellings, if you happen to misspell a word, or if you use a less common spelling. If you, for example, start typing *ggo*, when you want to type *google*, Google suggests a number of search terms beginning with google (Figure 1-11).

Figure 1-11   Google Suggest may correct spelling mistakes

- You may be offered to go directly to a specific site – bypassing the results pages – if Google finds this site to be particularly relevant to your search. For example, Google may suggest that you go directly to *www.amazon.com*, when you have typed *amaz* (Figure 1-12).

Figure 1-12   Google suggests you go directly to a site

- You may get suggestions based on your past searches. Until recently, this required that you were signed-in to your Google account (which means that you also had to have a Google account). Google has recently introduced a feature called Signed-out customization. This means that you now get suggestions based on your past searches, even when you don't have a Google account, and when you are not signed in. You can read more about customized search (also known as personalized search) below.

One of the most valuable things about the Google Suggest is that it assists you in writing precise, multi-word queries. When you continue to write your full search term, here *google search engine*, Google comes up with nine suggestions for specific queries with four or more words (Figure 1-13).

Figure 1-13   Google suggests specific queries

Google Suggest continues to work, when you search from the results page (Figure 1-14, page 22). In the example shown in Figure 1-14, we started by searching for the query *google search engine*. Google transfers the query to the search boxes on the results page. When you then start typing in one of the search boxes on the results page, Google suggests new queries. This gives you an option for refining your search, when you have seen the first results.

General and Personalized Query Suggestions

Query suggestions are primarily based on the general and recent popularity of various search terms. However, in addition, you may get personalized query suggestions in two situations.

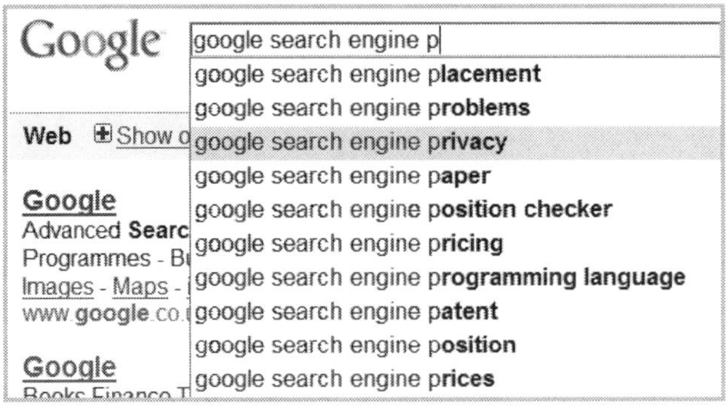

Figure 1-14 Google Suggest on a results page

Suggestions Based on Signed-in Search Activities

If you have a Google account and are signed-in, you get personalized suggestions based on your past search history. Google calls this your Web History. The Web History goes back to first time you signed in, unless you have deleted it at some later time. Suggestions based on signed-in search activities are outside the scope of this book and are not discussed further.

Suggestions Based on Signed-out Search Activities

If you don't have a Google account - or if you are not signed in to your account - Google may also give you personalized search suggestions. Google does this by storing all your signed-out search activities on their servers. The signed-out search activities are the searches you may when you don't have a Google account or when you are not signed-in to your account. Google links your search history to your PC by an anonymous browser cookie. The personalized query suggestions are based on your past 180 days searches. You can stop getting personalized suggestions when you are not signed in. Click on **Web History** in the top right corner on the results page (see Figure 2-1 N, page 62) to get to the Google Web History page. On this page, click **Disable customizations based on search activity** to turn off personalized suggestions, when you are not signed-in.

Google Suggest Drawbacks

Google Suggest is in general highly useful. However, you should realize that the suggestions are based on the general popularity and actuality of search terms. They may not be relevant to your current information needs.

This also applies when you get personalized suggestions (see above). The personalized suggestions are based on your past searches. If you are searching for information about a new topic, the personalized suggestions may not be useful.

The query suggestions you get may have a few flaws you should be aware of:

- At any given step (for each character typed), only the 10 most popular search terms are shown.
- You may overlook more relevant search terms coming up later, if you jump to a results page before you have finished typing.
- You may miss a relevant results page, if you jump directly to a specific Web page suggested by Google.
- You may be distracted from the query you are writing, when suggestions start coming up with other proposals.

Despite these minor flaws, Google Suggest is an excellent help for writing effective queries. We'll look at another example on page 36.

A First Glance at the Results Page

The remainder of this chapter will be used to discuss how you can get more relevant results. Before we go too deeply into this discussion, it may be a good idea to take a glance on the results page. The results you get, and the order, in which they are displayed, will tell you, if your search was successful. It is, therefore, important that you know how to read the results page, before we move on. In Chapter 2, we'll go through the results page in details.

The results are displayed on so-called results pages. Each page may display from 10, 20, 30, 50, or 100 results (see page 180). The standard setting is 10 results per page. This standard setting is used here, unless otherwise stated.

The Search Box

Figure 1-15 (page 24) shows a results page for the query *google web search*. On the results page, you find two search boxes, one on the top (Figure 1-15, A) of the page, and another at the bottom of the page (not shown in the figure). In each search box, your query, here *google web search*, is repeated. This makes it easy for you to refine your search, for example, by adding more keywords, removing keywords, or modifying keywords (by using alternative word forms, spellings, and so on). Most likely, you'll find that one of the easiest ways to get more relevant results is to add more keywords to your original query. Google Suggest offers great help for this (see Figure 1-14, page 22).

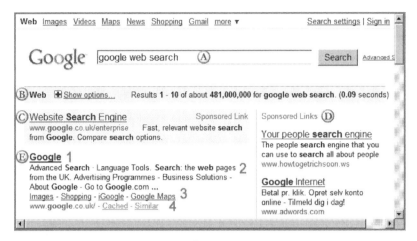

Figure 1-15   The basic anatomy of a results page

The Statistics Bar

The bar labeled B (Figure 1-15 B, and Figure 1-16) is often called the Statistics bar, because it gives you some statistics about your search. It also gives you some other information and access to the important Options panel (see below).

Figure 1-16   The Statistics bar

First, you are informed about which type of results you are looking at. In the example in Figure 1-16, Web means that the results page shows all results related to your keywords. Alternatively, you may choose to see only a subgroup of the results, for example, Images (see page 86 for further details).

Second, it gives you access to a number of options for refining and sorting your search results by various criteria. You get access to these options by clicking the **Show options** button. You then get to the Options

Panel. The Options Panel is described in details in the next chapter, starting on page 83.

Third, you are informed about the number of results displayed per page, here 10.

Last, you can see how many results Google found in response to your query, here 481,000,000. You can read more about the number of results on page 26. However, already here, I would like to inform you that you can "only" view up to 1,000 results for a given query.

Sponsored Links

Besides being an excellent search engine, Google Web Search is also a leading advertising platform. Google gets their main income from paid advertising. A paid ad on a Google results page is called a Sponsored link. You'll find two types of sponsored links on Google results pages. Above the search results, you may find up to three Sponsored links. They are shown on a yellow background and clearly labeled Sponsored link (Figure 1-15 C, page 24, and Figure 1-17).

Figure 1-17   Sponsored link above top results

Most often, there will be no or only one Sponsored link above the top results. You may also see Sponsored links to the right of your search results (Figure 1-15 D, and Figure 1-18). They are separated from the proper search results by a thin blue line and marked as Sponsored links on the top of the right column.

Figure 1-18   Sponsored link to the right of the search results

Search Results

Finally, you'll find what you are looking for, namely results of relevance to your query (Figure 1-15 E, page 24, and Figure 1-19). The relevant search results are presented as links to Web pages, also named documents. Each search result consists as a minimum of the following three elements:

- A link to the Web page with the information (Figure 1-19, 1). When you click on the link, you are taken to the Web page.
- A short summary of the Web page content – called a snippet (Figure 1-19, 2). By reading the snippet, you may get an idea about the relevance of the Web page.
- The Web page's URL address (Figure 1-19, 4).

Figure 1-19   A search result

You may also find some additional elements, for example:

- Links to relevant pages on the same site as the results page. In Figure 1-19, 3, there are links to *Images*, *Shopping*, *iGoogle*, and *Google Maps*. By clicking on these links, you get to Google's Image search, Google's Product search, the personalized home-page (iGoogle), and Google Maps, respectively.
- Links to Cached page and Similar pages (Figure 1-19, 4). You can read about Cached pages on page 65, and about Similar pages on page 66.

Number of Search Results

Google often finds a very high number of search results. In the example shown in Figure 1-5 (page 9) and Figure 1-15), our query was *google web search*. On Figure 1-5, you may be able to read that Google found 498,000,000 results! When the search was repeated a few days later, Google found "only" 481,000,000 results (Figure 1-15).

You shouldn't worry about the small difference in numbers of Web pages found. Google admits that the estimated number of results is not always accurate. In general, the number of search results for a given query increases over time, simply because people publish more and more on the Web. For topics of short-term intense interest, for example a major sport event, the number may go substantially up and down over time.

In any case, close to 500 million results are far too many. You wouldn't be able to access them all within a reasonable time. Most users seldom read more than the first 20 results. Many read or skim only the first few results.

This is why it is so important to use search techniques, which bring the most relevant results to the top of the results list.

The 1,000 Results Limit
Even if you were patient enough and had unlimited time, you wouldn't be able to browse through the 481,000,000 results. Google doesn't display more than 1,000 results for any query. You can test this out yourself. It's easier to do, if you first set the number of results to be displayed per page to 100 (see page 180). As an example, you may use the query *google web search* as in Figure 1-15 on page 24.

At the bottom of the results page, you find an indicator with numbers from 1 to 10 (Figure 1-20). We here call it the Page bar. You can read more about it on page 66.

Figure 1-20   Page bar with numbers 1 to 10

When you click on the last number 10, you would expect to see results number 901 to 1,000 (when you have set Google to display 100 results per page). You would also expect to be able to click the next blocks of 100 pages. Actually, this doesn't happen. Instead, when you click on 10 on the Page bar to see results number 901 to 1,000, the Statistics bar informs you that you - in this example - are viewing results number 701 – 776 of about 494,000,000 (Figure 1-21, page 28).

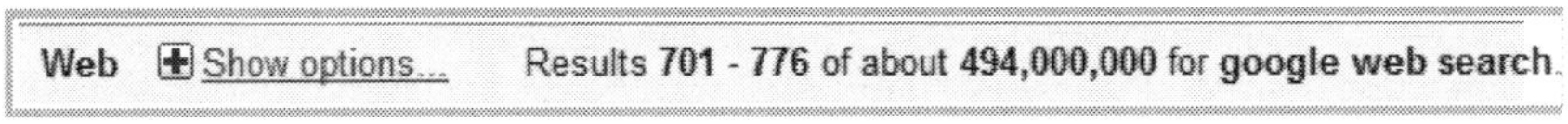

Web ⊞ Show options...   Results **701 - 776** of about **494,000,000** for **google web search**.

Figure 1-21   The last visible results for the query google web search

At the same time, the Page bar "shrinks" to display only the number from 1 to 8 – indicating that you can't view more than 800 results – at most (Figure 1-22). Note that the *Next* to the right of the numbers has disappeared from Figure 1-20 (page 27) to Figure 1-22.

Figure 1-22   Page bar after clicking 10 in Figure 1-20

Finally, at the bottom of the last results page, you get this message:

In order to show you the most relevant results, we have omitted some entries very similar to the 776 already displayed. If you like, you can re-peat the search with the omitted results included.

When you click on the hyperlinked part of the sentence shown (*repeat the search with the omitted results included*), Google displays some of the results not shown initially. If you continue to click on the last num-ber shown in the Page bar, you come to a point where Google simply doesn't display more results. The limit is set to 1,000 results. You may not always be able to achieve this limit – even if Google initially claimed to have found millions of pages of relevance to your query.

Web ⊞ Show options...   Results **901 - 1000** of about **386,000,000** for **google web search**.

Figure 1-23   Google displays a maximum of 1,000 results

You shouldn't see the 1,000 results limit as a problem. Only very few Web users would have the patience and the time needed to go through 1,000 results – not to talk about millions. If you don't find what you need within the first 10 to 50 results, you should refine your query. If you are like most people, it's unlikely you read more than the first few results or at most two or three pages of 10 results each. A study has shown that about 25% of the users only read the first few results – less than a whole page. Only 10% read more than the first three pages (cor-responding to 30 results).

The real challenge in Web search is to get fewer results of higher relevance. In the rest of this chapter, you'll be introduced to search techniques, which you may use to increase the number of relevant results at the top of the result where you'll notice them.

How Google Ranks Search Results

To improve your search technique and get results that are more relevant you need to have as basic knowledge about how the Google search engine works. We have already touched upon this topic in the section Write More Specific Queries When Needed (page 16). You'll now learn a little more about how the search engine scores Web pages and rank them. This may help you to make queries that are more effective, so you easier and faster find the results of most relevance to you.

Ranking of Web pages

Probably, the most important contribution to Web search that Google has made is a method for ranking of the search results – here meaning the total amount of relevant pages found.

Prior to the Google technique for ranking of relevant pages (known as PageRank) there was no method for getting the relevant pages ranked. Before, we had to rely on complex search queries using Boolean operators to try to separate the more relevant pages from the less relevant.

> **Introduction to Boolean operators**
> A Boolean operator is a command telling a search engine to find pages that contain all your keywords (the operator AND), at least one of them (the OR operator), or none of them (the operator NOT).
> Although some refinements were introduced, such as the possibility to search for exact phrases, queries based on Boolean operators can only find pages, which match your query. They don't provide any means for ranking the relevant pages found.
> Boolean search usually works well for structured databases with a limited number of documents, but is not well suited for searching the Web with billion of documents with no common structure. You get too many results.

Sergey Brin and Lawrence Page, the inventors of Google, introduced a ranking system, PageRank. The PageRank system ranks all pages on the Web. The PageRank for a page is based on the number and quality of the links to the page (see Popularity Score page 31 for more details). The PageRank, which we here call the popularity score, is given to the page solely based on the links to the page (inbound links). It is not dependent on your specific query. At any given time, every single page on the Web has a PageRank – if it has been visited by the Googlebot (see below).

The PageRank system is used to rank pages that Google has found to be relevant to your query. If Google didn't consider your query when ranking, you would always get the same list of results – displaying the most popular pages first. When you make a search, Google gives each page that matches your query a content score, also known as a relevance score. The content score given to a page is based on your query. The better your query matches the page's content, the higher content score the page will get (see Content Score page 31 for more details).

The Overall Score

Based on the specific content core (based on your query) and the general popularity score (based on the links to the page) each relevant page gets an overall score. The relevant pages are ranked by the overall score, so the pages with the highest overall scores are displayed first.

The difference between the popularity score and the content score is highly important, so let us try to summarize it here:

You can't do anything about the PageRank – the popularity score - when you make a search. The popularity score has been given to the Web pages before you start your search. It is not dependent on your query.

In contrast, you can do a lot for the content score. By writing effective queries (by using the guidelines given on page 11 to 18), you can significantly increase the content score for relevant pages. This way, relevant pages get a high overall ranking and get closer to the top of the results list.

Remember that the content score solely depends on the match between your query and the page's content. If you write queries with only one or two keywords, the Google search engine is most likely not able to give a high content score to any Web page. You don't give the Google search engine many chances to find out, what you specifically are looking for. As a result, it will have to rely primarily on the popularity score. This means that you'll get highly popular, but often not very relevant pages displayed on the top of the results list.

The Googlebot

The Google search engine contains a module or program called the Googlebot. The Googlebot constantly "crawls" the Web to find new pages and to revisit the pages it already knows. The pages are sent back to the Google databases. The essential information about the content of each page is extracted and stored in a content index (see Content Score below). The information about the links to and from the page is stored in a structure index.

Popularity Score

The popularity score is given to a Web page when the Google search engine finds and archives the page. It is regularly updated. The popularity score is based on the inbound links to the Web page.

Google uses an advanced set of rules for assigning a popularity score to a Web page. No one outside Google knows the rules in details. However, essentially, pages with many inbound links are given a higher popularity score than pages with fewer links. Furthermore, inbound links from more important pages are given higher weight than links from less important pages. The importance of a Web page is determined by a number of factors. In general, links from highly popular sites (google.com, cnn.com, and so on) are given more weight than links from less visited sites. Links from older sites are seen as more important than links from new sites. Also, links from pages with content related to the page are seen as more important than links from pages with irrelevant content. A number of additional factors not mentioned here are also used to assign a Web page its popularity score.

As mentioned above, the popularity score is calculated, before you enter your query. In contrast to the content score (see below), it doesn't depend on your query. It is said to be query-independent.

Content Score

When you make a query, the Google search engine finds the pages, which contains the query keywords. These pages are considered relevant to your query. The search engine gives each page a score called the content score.

The content score is given based on a complex set of rules. As for the popularity score, no one outside Google knows the rules in details. In general, pages where the keywords occur often, occur at important places (in particular titles and headings), and/or occur close to each other are given high content scores. In contrast, pages, where the keywords occur sparsely, occur at less important places, and/or occur widely separated from each other are given a lower content score.

The content score can first be calculated, when you have entered your query, and when Google search has found the relevant pages. This means that the content score – in contrast to the popularity score - depends on your query. It is said to be query-dependent.

The Search Engine Optimization Issue

If the score rules were known in their entirety, it would be easy for people wanting to get a top placement on the results page to optimize their homepage to be found and highly ranked by the Google search engine. Although the Google rules are not known in details, it is - to a certain extent - possible to design Web sites, so they are easily found, and so they get a relatively high rank. Of course, to attract visitors and to get inbound link a Web site needs to have some content of interest. To show up in your search results, they also need to be of some relevance to your query.

The discipline of optimizing Web sites to be found and to get as high rank as possible is called search engine optimization (SEO). There is a whole industry specializing in SEO. There is nothing wrong in optimizing a site to be found (as long as certain rules are obeyed). The problem is that many pages with relevant content – in relation to a given search query – may not be optimized to be found by search engines.

Many Web site owners may not be aware of the possibility to optimize their site for search engines, or they may not have the knowledge or time needed. Others are very good at this discipline. As a result, pages with similar relevance in relation to your search may get very different overall ranking. Some pages may be displayed on the top of the list, whereas other may not even be on the 1,000 results list.

As you'll see later in this chapter, it is of the utmost importance that you constantly keep in mind that many pages are designed to be found and to be highly rated. Especially, you should be aware that many pages with commercial content (which are not the same as paid ads, see page 82) are well structured and often optimized to be attractive the Googlebot, so they can get a high PageRank. For this reason, you may easily get many pages with high popularity score and little relevance on the top of the results list. This is especially true, if you query only contains one or two general keywords.

The most important challenge in Web search today is to learn how to by-pass the high number of popular, but irrelevant pages, so you get directly to the pages of interest for your query. This is not an art, but a craft you can learn relatively easily by following and practicing the techniques described in the book.

Getting the Most Relevant Pages to the Top

Just to sum up: The most important thing you can do to get the most relevant pages to the top of the results list is to increase the content score. Keep in mind that the content score is based on your query. The more complete, accurate, and specific you write your query, the higher the content score will be for pages of relevance to your query. This way, pages with highly relevant content have a good chance to outperform popular pages with less relevant content. When you master to write queries that increases the content score you can start thinking about how to refine the search by using filters. Again, remember that use of filters and other tools is not a substitute for a good query but a valuable supplement to be used for fine-tuning of your search.

Evaluating the Relevance of the Results

Only you can judge the relevance of the results you get. When you have made a search, you should always carefully review the first 10 to 20 results to see if they meet your expectations. Actually, it often happens that the results of your first query don't give you the information you need. There may be several reasons for this:

- When you start, you often don't have a firm idea about what to search for.
- You may not know the words most accurately describing your topic.
- You may have omitted some words, which turn out be important for the information you need.
- You may find that some people use other terms for the topic than you do.
- You may realize you need more background information to write an effective query.

For these reasons, the results of your first query may sometimes just serve as an inspiration for you how to make a better search.

You shouldn't worry, if your first query doesn't lead to the information you need. You'll be learning as you go. This is actually the way, which seems most natural for us, when we search for information. For each new piece of information you find, you learn more, get new inspiration, and modify your search to find more information of higher relevance. At each stage, you most likely learn something valuable.

Quality of the Results

When you find information on the Web, you should keep in mind that the Web is an open society. In many countries, people with access to a computer and the Internet can publish almost everything they want on the Web. There are practically no limits to the type or amount of documents, which can be uploaded to the Web. With few exceptions, there is no quality review of the documents prior to publishing. There is no central organization responsible for classifying, organizing, or maintaining the information on the Web. Therefore, the criteria traditionally used to assess the quality of information may not be well suited to evaluate the quality of Web information.

Most likely, there is no simple, general method for evaluation of the quality of Web information. It is outside the scope of this book to go further into approaches and methods, which might be applicable to such an evaluation. You'll get a few advices in later chapters. In general, you have to rely on your common sense. And it is never a bad idea to maintain a sound skepticism when surfing the Web!

How to Get More Relevant Results

If you don't find the results you expect or need, you must first try to identify the problem. There is no general method for this, but asking a few simple questions often helps. The two most fundamental questions are:

- Am I getting too many or too few results?
- Am I getting some relevant results at all - or are they all irrelevant?

The most common problem is that you get far too many results of low or no relevance. More seldom, you get a reasonably number of results, but too few or no relevant results. You may also get no results at all. Below, we first look at how you can focus your search, if you get too many results. Later, you learn how to expand your search, if you get no results at all or too few relevant results.

Focusing Your Search

If you get too many results of low or no relevance, you most likely need to focus your search. To do this, you have to describe your query in more details. As we have already discussed (see How to Write a Query, page 11, and Write More Specific Queries When Needed, page 16), you should in general write queries with four or more keywords, try to search for exact phrases, and use words that precisely describe your topic. In addition, you may have to enforce Google to exclude unwanted words. You may also want to use one or more filters to restrict your search, for example to a specific filetype, a specific site, or a specific date.

In summary, the most important methods you have at your disposal to further focus your search are:

- Use additional keywords
- Search for exact phrases
- Eliminate unwanted words
- Use filters (filetype, site, date, and so on)

We have already briefly discussed the first two methods. Below, we go into more details. In addition, you get an introduction to the last two methods - eliminating unwanted words and using filters.

Using Additional Keywords

A few years ago, most people used only one or two keywords per query. Today, the queries are becoming somewhat longer. However, according to a recent report (November 2009) by Trellian/KeywordDiscovey, about 65% of queries in the US are still only one or two keywords. In many other countries, queries with one or two keywords are even more frequent. For example, about 75% of the queries in Sweden have only one or two keywords. Queries with three or more keywords are still infrequently used. In the US, only 19% of the queries have three keywords. Queries with four or more keywords make up less than 16% in the US. In the other 12 countries, for which the search statistics is shown in the report, queries with four or more keywords make up even less - with the exception of Poland, where it is about 18%.

Queries with more than 10 keywords represent less than 0.3% of all queries. You can see the detailed report and current statistics on:

http://www.keyworddiscovery.com/keyword-stats.html

If we assume it takes at least four keywords to describe a search topic adequately, the statistics described above means that more than 80% of the Web users worldwide could improve their search habits just by writing longer queries (consisting of relevant keywords, of course)!

Building Long Queries

Use of long queries – here defined as four keywords or more – is probably one of the most effective ways to improve the content score and thereby to get the relevant results to the top of the results list. Of course, you need to use appropriate keywords. Here, your knowledge of the topic will be of great help. As stated above, even though you don't know the topic of your interest very well initially, your searches will soon increase your knowledge. However, until you get that far, you may benefit from using Google Suggest (see also page 18).

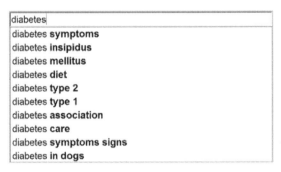

Figure 1-24   Query suggestions for the keyword diabetes

Get Assistance from Google Suggest

Google Suggest is a great source of inspiration, when building queries. However, keep its minor flaws in mind.

- Most importantly, for each character you type, it only shows the 10 most common or popular search terms (Figure 1-24). Many terms and keywords, which may be of interest for your search, are not shown. You can easily get access to some of these by typing a space after the word shown in the search box followed by a letter (or number) as shown in the example below (Figure 1-25, page 37).

- Google only suggests the most popular search terms. It may not show the term of most interest to you. You can work around this weakness by using the suggestions to build your own query. Often, the suggestions will give you a good idea about the key terms used within your topic.

In the example below, we illustrate the use of Google Suggest to build a query related to the topic *diabetes*.

1. We start by typing *diabetes* (Figure 1-24, page 36). Already here you learn that there are different types of diabetes (insipidus, mellitus, type 1, and type 2). For your information, diabetes insipidus is a disease, which is not related to the common diabetes. The common diabetes with too much sugar in the blood and urine is diabetes mellitus, which exists in two major types, Type 1 and Type 2.
2. Apparently, there are no search term suggestions starting with *b*, *e*, *f*, or several of the other 26 letters (Figure 1-24). Actually, Google has suggestions for search terms starting with each letter. If you, for example, want to see search terms starting with *t*, just enter a space and *t* after *diabetes* (Figure 1-25). You now get suggestions for such important search terms as *diabetes testing* and *diabetes treatment*.

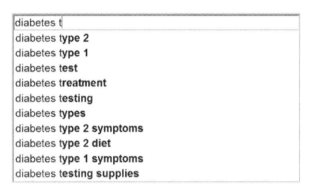

Figure 1-25   Query suggestions for the term diabetes t

3. Let us assume you want to know something about *diabetes treatment*. You could click directly on *diabetes treatment*. However, this way you would miss the more detailed proposals for search terms for *diabetes treatment*. Unless you want a broad overview of *diabetes treatment*, a better practice is to scroll down to the search term of interest, here *diabetes treatment*. Don't press Enter. Google now writes the search term in the search box (Figure 1-26, page 38).

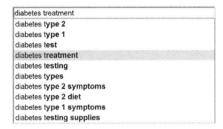

Figure 1-26 Scrolling to the search term diabetes treatment

4. You now get 10 new suggestions (Figure 1-27). As in point 2 above, you can get new suggestions by entering a space followed by a letter of your choice. In this example, Google has new proposals for most of the letters. If you, for example, enter *s*, one of the suggestions is *diabetes treatment side effects* (Figure 1-28).

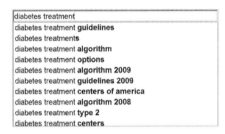

Figure 1-27 Query suggestions for the term diabetes treatment

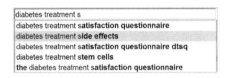

Figure 1-28 Query suggestions for the term diabetes treatment s

5. At this point, Google doesn't suggest any more queries. In general, Google doesn't seem to suggest queries longer than eight keywords, but there may be some examples on longer queries. During the process of building a query with assistance from Google Suggest, you learn a number of key terms related to your topic. In this example, you have met such important key terms as *diabetes treatment options*, *diabetes treatment type 2*, and *diabetes treatment side effects*. From these key terms, you could build queries such as *di-*

abetes type 2 treatment options or *diabetes type 2 treatment side effects* - or even more detailed and precise queries, if you wanted.

Searching for Exact Phrases

Google by itself does a good job in finding document, where the keywords you specific occur close to each other. Documents where the keywords occur close to each other are given a higher content score than documents where the keywords are more spread out. However, often you can get the relevant results higher up on the results list by specifying that some or all the keywords must occur in a specific sequence - as an exact phrase. Google then only finds the documents, where the keywords occur exactly as you have typed them. Even so-called stopwords (see page 50) are included.

What does Google say about use of quotation marks?

Google says that quotation marks are usually unnecessary: *By putting double quotes around a set of words, you are telling Google to consider the exact words in that exact order without any change. Google already uses the order and the fact that the words are together as a very strong signal and will stray from it only for a good reason, so quotes are usually unnecessary. By insisting on phrase search you might be missing good results accidentally. For example, a search for ["Alexander Bell"] (with quotes) will miss the pages that refer to Alexander G. Bell.*

I partly agree, but you should be aware of the following aspects:

1. Google looks for order and closeness of the words. This is similar to, but not identical to searching for an exact phrase, as practice will show you.
2. Google uses the term "usually". For practical purposes, this means that you can't know when you need to search for an exact phrase.
3. Google apparently focuses on the risk for overlooking a good result, when the real challenge in general seems to be to get rid of the many irrelevant results.

Having said this, I find that Google usually places results where the words occur as an exact phrase high on the results list. However, sometimes you can improve the relevance of the results further by instructing Google to look specifically for an exact phrase by enclosing the words within quotation marks. The only way to find out, if you may benefit from searching for an exact phrase, is by carrying out your search with and without quotation marks around the exact phrase, you want to find.

To get Google to find only documents where some or all the keywords occur as an exact phrase (in a specific sequence), enclose the keywords or phrase within quotation marks as in *"google web search"* (Figure 1-29).

```
"google web search"
```

Figure 1-29   Search for the exact phrase google web search

In this example, the "noise reduction" was quite remarkable. Whereas the query *google web search* gave about 500 million results, the query for the exact phrase *"google web search"* gave less than 4 millions. However, the first 20 results were almost identical. The order of the 20 results was a little different. In this case, there was no notable increase in the relevance of the results.

For other queries, the number of results is dramatically reduced, and the relevant results are displayed on the first few results pages. This makes it easy to skim through the results and to find the most relevant ones. We saw an example on the benefit of searching for exact phrases in the box on page 13.

Only the first 20 results really matter!
A study has shown that as many as 62% of the people only read the first 10 results – at most. Other studies have come to similar conclusions. This emphasize why it is so important to eliminate the irrelevant results and to get the most relevant results to the top of the results list.
As a consequence, I only look at the first 20 results, when I evaluate, if different queries or different search methods give different results.

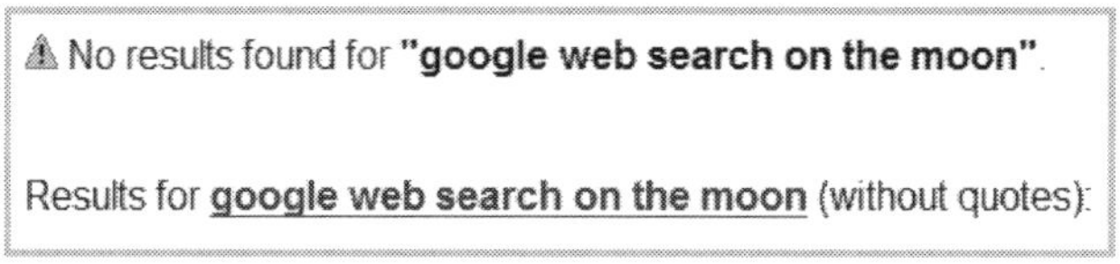

⚠ No results found for **"google web search on the moon"**.

Results for **google web search on the moon** (without quotes):

Figure 1-30   Search for a non-existing exact phrase

If the exact phrase doesn't exist in Google's document database, you'll be informed that no results were found. As an example, the query *"google web search on the moon"* gave no results (Figure 1-30, page 40).

Google then instead displays the results found without quotes (not shown in the figure).

Obviously, search for a non-existing exact phrase doesn't improve the relevance of the search results in any way. It is, therefore, important that you only enclose "meaningful" sequences of words within quotation marks. To do this, try to think about how the words are used in natural, spoken language. Most people write Web documents this way.

Queries with More Than One Exact Phrase

If your query contains many words, you may occasionally benefit from having more than one exact phrase in the query. Let us as an example assume that we wanted to know something about how Google Web Search ranks results. For this purpose, we could specify our first query *"google web search"* further by adding *ranking of results*. As shown in the table below the query *google web search ranking of results* gave 11,500,000 results, whereas search for the two exact phrases *"google web search"* and *" ranking of results"* gave only 53 results. Also, note that the inclusion of the "stopword" *of* reduced the number of results – both with and without quotation marks. Google often does include stopwords in the search – despite many claims to the contrary (page 50).

Query	Results
google web search ranking of results	11,500,000
"google web search" ranking of results	19,100
"google web search" ranking results	71,600
"google web search" "ranking results"	376
"google web search" "ranking of results"	53

Be aware that the number of results shown in the table above and in other examples in the book is a snapshot. It shows how the situation was the day the test was made. If you repeat the test at a later date, you may get different results. The results shown in the table are from a search made March 28, 2010. When I first made the search, I only got 1,480,000 results for the query without quotation marks. However, the numbers of results for the query *"google web search" "ranking of results"* were almost identical in the two tests (53 versus 52 previously).

Benefits of Using Exact Phrase Queries

As you saw in the box on page 39, Google says that search for an exact phrase (by enclosing the keywords in quotation marks) is usually not necessary. While this may be partly true, you can't really use it for anything, because you don't know, if this applies for your particular query. If you don't get the relevant results you are looking for, you should always try to enclose any keywords that are part of an exact phrase within quotation marks.

If there is more than one exact phrase in your query, you should try searching for one exact phrase at a time. When you have tried this and assessed, if it increases the relevance of the results, you may try to search for two exact phrases at the same time. Search for two exact phrases at a time may be highly effective. However, be aware that search for two exact phrases often dramatically reduces the number of results. In this situation, there is a real risk that you may miss some relevant results.

Whether it increases the relevance of the results or not to search for exact phrases, depends on, what you are searching for. As stated, you have to try it out to see, if searching for exact phrases adds any value.

Eliminating Unwanted Words

You may now and then benefit from excluding some words from your search. This may, for example, be the case if Web pages offering products or services for sale dominate your search results. If you are looking for technical information, you may want to reduce the number of such results. Google offers various methods for doing this.

You may use the Advanced Search form. It includes a "search box" for words you want to exclude (Figure 3-4, A4, page 110). We here call it the exclude search box. Alternatively, you can use the minus (-) operator. Just put a minus sign (-) in front of each unwanted word. Don't put a space between the minus sign and the word to be eliminated. You can read about the use of the minus (-) operator on page 145.

You can use the exclude search box on the Advanced Search form and the minus operator to exclude all types of results. If you just want to reduce the number of commercial pages (shopping sites), it may be better to select the option Fewer shopping sites on the Options panel (page 101).

Instead of using the exclude search box or the minus operator to exclude unwanted words, it may be a better search practice to specify positively, which information you want to find by using some of the other methods we have discussed.

Note that you can't use the exclude search box or the minus operator alone. They can only be used to exclude some words in a query where you are searching for something else. You may also use the minus operator in combination with the plus operator to search for a specific word form or a specific spelling of a word (see example page 145).

Using Filters

Google Web Search comes with many tools for filtering the search results. Filtering means that you select a subgroup of the search results. You thereby also filter out other results. The Google people say that you restrict or limit your search (to a certain subgroup of results). In this book, the words filter, filter out, restrict, and limit are used with the same meaning.

Use of filters is an effective way to increase the relevance of your search results. However, keep in mind that use of filters is not a substitute for writing a good query. Filters are best seen as a valuable supplement to good queries – not as a substitute for an effective query. Sometimes, you may need to use filters just to get the number of results down to a level you can handle – even when you start out with an effective query. Filters are also very useful for guiding the search into a specific direction – for example to specific subgroups of results such as sites or filetypes (see below).

As you'll learn later, you may combine many of the filters. By adding a combination of filters to an effective query, you often easily find the information you need.

The more important ways to filter the search results are listed below. An example of the use of each filter is given in the parenthesis following the description of the filter. You'll find detailed information about how to use the individual filters and how to combine them effectively in later chapters.

Filters may be used for restricting your search to:

- Web pages in a specific language (French)
- A specific filetype (.pdf)
- A specific domain (.gov) or site (google.com)
- A date range (June 1, 2009, to July 31, 2009)
- A time period (last week)
- A specific part of the web pages (title)

- A specific region (France)
- A numeric range (50 – 100)
- Usage rights (free to use or share)
- Content type (strict filtering)

You can use different methods to filter the results. Use of the Advanced Search form (Chapter 3) is probably the easiest and best way to use filters. First, you get easy access to most of the filters. Second, you can only use combinations of filters, which the search engine accepts, so you don't risk combining filters, which cancel each other out. Third, you get good help how to use the filters on the form. Last, you don't have to learn about the advanced search operators (Chapter 4) that may be used to replace some of the Advanced Search form's functions.

Besides these "classic" filters, Google also offers you a number of other methods to filter or see the results. The more important options are listed below. Among other things, you can limit the search results to:

- Images
- Videos
- News
- Blogs
- Books
- Discussions

The easiest way to get access to these filters is to use the Options panel (also known as the Options menu). Google has recently greatly expanded and improved the Options panel. The Options panel gives you access to a number of filtering possibilities, which are not easily available by other means. The additional filtering possibilities offered by the Options panel are a great supplement to the filter options on the Advanced Search form (to be described in Chapter 3). You can read about the Options panel in Chapter 2, page 83 to 103.

Expanding Your Search

Even though you usually get too many results, it may actually happen that you get too few! You may get no results at all, or you may get some, but the few you find are not relevant. The web contains billions of documents. With this number of documents, you should think that there would always be some documents, which would satisfy your information need. This is also almost always the case. However, for various reasons your query may not always find them.

Why You May Get too Few Results - and What to Do

For the discussion below, we exclude the possibility that you have used operators incorrectly – except for a small typo (a missing space). Some of the more common reasons you get too few results are:

- Non-existing keywords or serious misspellings
- Lack of space between an operator and a keyword
- Inappropriate use of quotation marks
- Use of too many keywords
- Use of too specific keywords

We look closer at each of these potential errors below.

Non-existing Words or Serious Misspellings

If you make misspellings, Google usually discovers this and informs you about the problem (see page 56). In some cases, Google may not be able to guess the correct spelling. As a result, Google can't give you any advice as to how to spell the keyword correctly. In this situation, Google doesn't display any results, but gives you a warning (Figure 1-31).

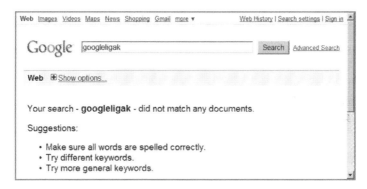

Figure 1-31   Queries for non-existing words give no results

Lack of Space after an Operator

When we come to the more advanced stuff later in the book, you learn how to use operators. We have already briefly looked at the minus operator (page 42). Operators are used together with keywords in the search box. Correct use of spaces in relation to operators is of vital importance to ensure they work correctly. You'll learn the rules later. Here we just look at errors that may occur if you forget a space. In the example below, I have used the OR operator. You can read about the OR operator on page 48 later in this chapter.

If the keywords are relatively common, Google often detects the missing space and suggests the correct alternative. In the example shown in Figure 1-32, Google guessed I meant *callable OR mortgage* – not *callable ORmortgage*. (For your information, the two terms, callable and mortgage, are commonly used together in relation to bonds).

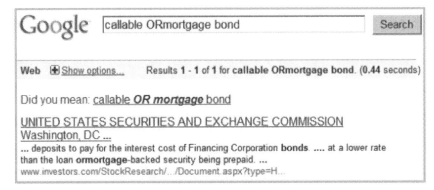

Figure 1-32   Google guesses I missed a space after OR

For rarely used words, Google may not be able to guess that you may have forgotten a space after the operator. In the example shown in Figure 1-33 (page 47), Google didn't guess I meant duration OR convexity. (For your information, the two terms are both related to bonds, but the term convexity is only used by specialists).

Google here gives you're a more detailed warning than in Figure 1-31 (page 45). You also get suggestions how to resolve the error. However, you are not told that you just missed a space. Putting the space in place will give you about 10 million results!

Inappropriate Use of Quotation Marks
As you have seen, inclusion of a sequence of words within quotation marks may sometime improve the relevance of the results (page 39). However, the risk with this approach is that the query may become too specific.

If you happen to search for a non-existing phrase, Google gives you a warning. The search results found without the quotation marks are also displayed.

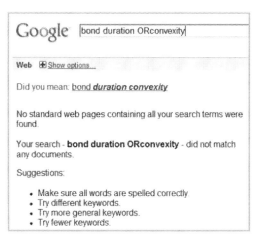

Figure 1-33   Google didn't guess I missed a space after OR

Use of Too Many Keywords

As we have seen, long queries with appropriate and specific keywords are a powerful tool for getting highly relevant results. However, as for use of quotation marks, there is a risk of overdoing. In this situation, Google doesn't give you a warning. You have to figure out yourself that you have made a query that is too specific. You have to go back again and remove one or more keywords. Remember that this doesn't need to be the last keyword you added. Try to identify the keyword, which restrict the search the most. You may do this by eliminating one word at a time and look at the results.

Use of Too Specific Keywords

If you use keywords, which are too specific, you don't get any warning from Google. You have to figure this out yourself. Try to identify the keyword or keywords, which are most likely responsible for the limited number of results. Try to think about what words other people may use. And try to use more common and general words. You may benefit from using a thesaurus. Alternatively, you may use Google's built-in tool to search for synonyms. It is known as the tilde operator (~). If use of synonyms doesn't solve the problem, you may also try to use the wildcard operator (*) for one keyword at a time. The use of the tilde (~) operator and the wildcard operator (*) are described on page 48 and page 49, respectively.

General Tools for Getting More Results

You have just learned how to correct specific "errors", which may lead to too few results. In this section, we are going to look at some more general tools to expand your search. They may be useful, if your first query resulted in too few results, and you didn't make any of the errors described above. You may also benefit from these tools, if you find your topic was not covered well enough by the results. If you decide to use these tools, be careful not to go to the other extreme. Too generous use of in particular the wildcard operator (*) easily leads to too many results. Getting the right amount of results, which are relevant and cover the topic sufficiently, takes some skills. You'll acquire the needed skills by reading the rest of the book – and by practicing.

Including Synonyms in the Search

Google sometimes includes synonyms in the search, even though you don't ask it to do so. Google's "automatic" use of synonyms is neither predictable nor controllable. First, you can't foresee, when Google will include synonyms in the search. Second, you can't control, which synonyms Google includes.

Use of the Tilde Operator (~)

To work around the first of these weaknesses, you can enforce Google Web Search to include synonyms when and where you want it. You do this by putting a tilde sign (~) in front of the keyword, for which you want to include synonyms.

You need to put a tilde operator in front of each keyword, for which you want Google to include synonyms in the search. Don't overuse the tilde operator. If you use it for more than one keyword per query, you easily end up with a query, which is not sufficiently specific.

Use of a tilde in front of a keyword doesn't necessarily prevent Google to include synonyms for other keywords as well. More importantly, you still don't get any control over which synonyms Google uses. To get more control over the use of synonyms, you need to use the OR operator (described in the next section) and to choose the synonyms yourself.

Use of the OR Operator

The OR operator is a highly versatile and effective tool. You can use it to include well-defined alternatives to your primary keywords in your search. Among other things, you can use it to:

48

- include synonyms to one or more keywords in a controlled way
- search for different concepts covering essentially the same information need
- include alternative grammatical word forms in the query
- include alternative spellings of a keyword in a controlled way
- look for more than one file type in the same query

When you start making more advanced searches, you'll probably find the OR operator to be a highly valuable tool. You can read more about the use of the OR operator to include synonyms on page 147.

Including Undefined Words in the Search

You may want to search for any possible word in a given position. Let us assume your query consists of three keywords, *keyword 1*, *keyword 2*, and *keyword 3*. You are uncertain about which keyword would be the best in the second position (*keyword 2*). In this situation, you can leave it to Google to look for any possible word. You do this by using the wildcard operator instead of a specific keyword as described below.

The Wildcard Operator (*)
The wildcard operator is entered as an asterisk (*). It replaces one or more words. The wildcard operator expands your search substantially more than the OR operator does. Use of the wildcard operator carries a substantial risk of making the search too broad and getting too many irrelevant results. The wildcard operator is often best used as a replacement for a single word in a sequence such as *three * men*.

Note, that the wildcard operator in Google only can replace one or more words – not a character. In many database search engines, you may use one symbol, for example a question mark (?), to replace a single character in a word, and another symbol, often *, to replace several characters in a word. In Google, you can't use a symbol to replace one or more characters in a word. The wildcard operator can only replace one or more whole words. You don't need worry about this. Google's spelling corrections and use of stemming (see page 53) make use of symbols to replace individual characters superfluous and offer better alternatives.

Other Important Search features

In the next three sections, we are going to look at three important search features: stopwords, stemming, and spell corrections. They are not related to each other. Although they only seldom need any action from you, you may benefit from having a basic knowledge about how they work and how they may affect your search.

Stopwords

The term stopword is misleading. A stopword doesn't stop the search – or anything else. A stopword is simply a word that is - or may be - ignored by Google. A more appropriate term would be "ignored word" or "common word". However, the accepted and commonly used term is stopword.

Stopwords are Words that May be Ignored

Stopwords may be defined as words that are so common, so it wouldn't pay off to include them in the search. They are said to be ignored by the search engine if you include them in your query. Examples on possible stopwords are *to*, *be*, *or*, *not*. Because these words are so common, in most cases it wouldn't improve the relevance of the results to include them in the search. Seen from Google's side, inclusion of such words would increase the indices of stored words substantially. This would increase the costs of operating the many servers running Google Web Search. It could also potentially slow down the search engine's response time. So until recently (see the box below), the common wisdom was that stopwords are better left out.

Some Stopwords May be Meaningful

The Google people obviously know that common words may be meaningful in some situations. They have done some very good work to engineer the search engine, so it includes stopwords in the search, when this is meaningful. Meaningful here implies that the relevance of the search results is increased, when the stopwords are included in the search.

How does Google determine that a stopword is meaningful?
Probably, nobody outside Google knows exactly how Google decides when to include stopwords in the search. However, you may get a good clue from Google's patent "Locating meaningful stopwords or stop-phrases in keyword-based retrieval systems", US Patent 7,409,383. In one variation of this invention, Google first looks for stopwords in your search query in its list of potential stopwords. If it finds potential stopwords, it carries out a search with all the keywords you entered - including any potential stopwords. It

also carries out a search excluding the potential stopwords in your query. Finally, the search engine compares the results from the two searches. If the two sets of results found are not substantially similar, it concludes that the stopwords are meaningful in relation to your search and display the results for your query including the meaningful stopwords.

Use of the Plus (+) Operator to Include Stopwords

You may enforce Google to include a potential stopword by putting a + sign in front of the word. There should be no space between + and the keyword. If you, for example, enter the query *+to +be +or +not +to +be*, you enforce Google to include *to*, *be*, *or* and *not* in the search. These four words are often ignored by Google. However, in this case, it is not needed to tell Google to include *to*, *be*, *or* and *not* in the search. You could just as well enter *to be or not to be*. Google "knows" this is a famous phrase from William Shakespeare's play Hamlet (Figure 1-34)

In summary, you usually don't need to put a + sign in front of possible stopwords in your search query. You should only enforce Google to include a stopword, if you think it may increase the relevance of the results. If you are in doubt, if a stopword matters, you can just test it out by searching with and without a plus sign before the word.

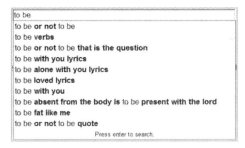

Figure 1-34   Query suggestions for to be

How to See When Google Includes Stopwords

You can see if Google includes a potential stopword or not. You may get two clues. You often get the first clue already when you start entering your keywords. If Google "knows" a stopword and plans to include it in the search, Google may suggest the stopword in the query suggestions – if it is popular enough. As an example, let us take the search phrase *to be* (Figure 1-34). Google here suggests 10 search phrases beginning with *to be*. This shows that Google will include the "stop-phrase" *to be* in the search - at least for some phrases. If you continue typing, you'll even get a hint that the phrase *to be or not to be* occur in the Hamlet play (Figure 1-35).

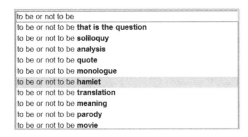

Figure 1-35   Query suggestions for to be or not to be

You get the second clue on the results page. When Google includes a stopword in the search, the stopword is – as any other word included in the search – displayed in bold type (**To be, or not to be**) (Figure 1-36).

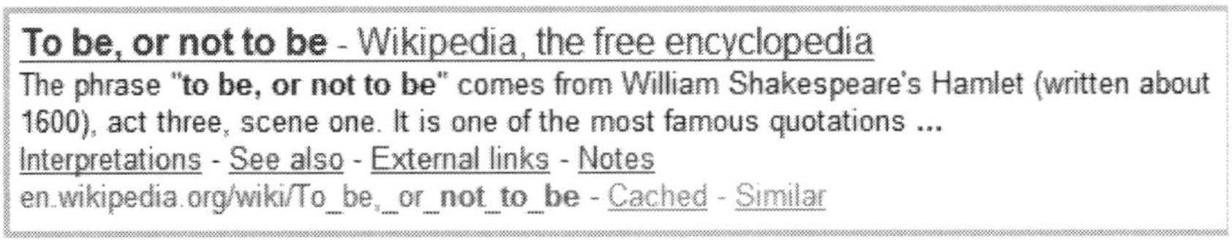

To be, or not to be - Wikipedia, the free encyclopedia
The phrase "**to be, or not to be**" comes from William Shakespeare's Hamlet (written about 1600), act three, scene one. It is one of the most famous quotations ...
Interpretations - See also - External links - Notes
en.wikipedia.org/wiki/To_be,_or_**not**_**to**_**be** - Cached - Similar

Figure 1-36   Words included in the search are displayed in bold

Searching for Different Word Forms

Typically, we search only for one form of a keyword. Most of the words we use in our language exist in several different grammatical forms (called inflections by language specialists). Often, different word forms – or at least some of them - are spelled differently. To be sure to find the results of interest to you, you may benefit from knowing a little about how Google stores the different word forms in its databases.

About Different Forms of the Same Word

We start with a bit of grammatical information. If English is your native language, or if you know English well, you can skip this section.

Nouns in English can be singular or plural. Modern English has no grammatical gender (masculine, feminine, or neuter). Depending on its function in a sentence, a noun may exist in four cases: nominative, accusative, genitive, and dative. In English, the noun is spelled identical in nominative, accusative, and dative. The genitive exists in the form of 's for the singular genitive (as in cat's) or just an apostrophe ' for plural genitive (as in cats'). When we write a query for a noun, we thus only need to consider four forms. The four forms are listed below (with an example in parenthesis):

- Nominative singular (*cat*)
- Nominative plural (*cats*)
- Genitive singular (cat's)
- Genitive plural (*cats'*)

Verbs can exist in different tenses such as present, past and future. Fortunately, the formation of the tenses in English is simple – at least from a search point of view. When we write a query, we only need to consider four (differently spelled) forms of regular verbs. As an example, the four forms of the regular verb *bake* are:

- Bake – the infinitive
- Bakes – the third person singular present tense
- Baked – the perfect tense
- Baking – the –ing form

For irregular (strong) verbs, there may be five forms to consider, for example (to) drink, drinks, drank, drunk, and drinking.

Google Uses Stemming to Find Word Forms

When you enter a keyword, you might also be interested in finding documents containing other forms of the same word. If you, for example, want to search for the keyword *bake*, you may also be interested in documents with one or more of the words *bakes*, *baked*, and *baking*.

Search engines can use three different methods to expand your keywords to cover different forms of the same word. Language experts call these methods:

- Truncation
- Stemming
- Lemmatization

Google uses stemming. We are not going to discuss truncation or lem-matization in details here. However, you should know that Google doesn't "understand" or use truncation the way, you might know from other search engines. This means that you shouldn't attempt to use a symbol such as ? or * to substitute for any part of a word. In Google, the wildcard operator * may only be used for one or more words – not for a part of the word (see page 49). You shouldn't see the lack of the trunca-tion feature in Google as a weakness. When you search on the web, use of truncation would usually result in far too many irrelevant results.

How Stemming Works

Stemming tries to reduce the different grammatical forms of a keyword to a common term – the stem or root. For example, stemming reduces the keywords *bake*, *bakes*, *baked*, and *baking* to the stem *bake*. This means that whichever of the four word forms occur in a document (on a Web page), it is stored as the same word, the stem *bake*, in Google's keyword databases. The advantage for the search engine is that less space is used to store the information about keyword occurrence in the billions of documents on the Web. For you as a user it has – at least in theory – the advantage that you don't necessarily have to search for different forms of grammatically closely related word forms.

Stemming is done by a mathematical program, called an algorithm. There are several algorithms for stemming. The commonly used algo-rithms work somewhat similar to truncation. They remove the ending of the keyword. However, whereas truncation only offers you the possibili-ty to remove a number of characters from the word (usually from the end), stemming works by removing endings by use of grammatical rules. For example, the program will know when to remove the ending –s from the third person singular (runs) to get to the stem (run) and when to remove –es (for example, *washes* → *wash*). Stemming removes the end-ings in a more meaningful way than you would be able to by using trun-cation. Furthermore, the whole stemming process runs automatically.

Stemming results in expansion of your keyword in the sense that the search engine also may display pages, which contain other forms of your keyword than the one you entered. For example, when you search for bake, Google may in addition list pages containing *bakes*, *baked* and *baking*. All word forms, which Google includes in the search, are dis-played in bold. To see an example, try searching for *bake*. When I did this, I found the word forms *bake*, *baked*, and *baking* in the first 10 documents. As we'll see later, stemming doesn't necessarily lead to results, which are more relevant.

How Google's Stemming Works

As stated above, the Google search engine uses stemming. Google has not published how their stemming program works. It is, therefore, not precisely known how stemming is used for the various word classes. The general opinion seems to be that the Google search engine stems relatively well for the singular and plural forms of nouns.

To evaluate how well Google's stemming works for nouns, you may, for example, try to search for the four forms of the noun cat (*cat, cats, cat's, and cats'*, see also page 53). Try first to search for each form at a time. You may then try to search for all four forms at the same time by using the query *cat OR cats OR cat's OR cats'*.

People are less certain how it deals with verb tenses. To evaluate how well Google's stemming works for verbs, you may, for example, try to search for the five forms of the irregular verb drink (*drink, drinks, drank, drunk, drinking*, see also page 53). Try first to search for each form at a time. You may then try to search for all five forms at the same time by using the query *drink OR drinks OR drank OR drunk OR drinking*.

I think it is fair to say that Google in general does a good stemming job. Google's intention seems to be to avoid stemming too much. Overuse of stemming, for example, by including adjectives (such as doable) derived from verbs (do) might easily result in too many search results of low or no relevance.

However, if you have carried out the small experiments suggested above, I guess you may agree that it sometimes may be worth searching for individual grammatical forms of a keyword (see also below).

Search for a Specific Word Form

Although Google in general does a good stemming job, as shown above, you can't fully rely on it. To find specific word forms, you may need to enter exactly the word form you are looking for. If you know - or suspect - that a specific form of the word is more likely to be used in the relevant documents, you may benefit from starting with this word. For example, you get very different results for a query starting with *drunk* compared with a query starting with *drink*. In the first case, you find a lot of results about alcohol intoxication. In the latter case, you primarily find results related to how to prepare drinks.

You can read on page 146 to 147 how you can use the OR operator to enforce Google to include different word forms in your search. The benefit of using the OR operator is that you getter better control over, which word forms to be include in your search. The disadvantage could be that you might miss some of the word forms, Google would include as results of its own stemming. However, you don't need to worry about this. Use of the OR operator doesn't prevent Google from applying its own stemming. The stemmed word forms are already built into Google's database. The only real risk of using the OR operator is that you may get too many results of low relevance.

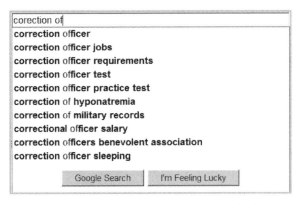

Figure 1-37   Google suggests you may have misspelled a word

Corrections of Misspellings

According to Google, many queries contain misspelled words. If Google thinks you may have made a misspelling, it tries to assist you correcting it. You may get a hint from Google Suggest that you are misspelling a word already when you are typing it (Figure 1-37). In the example shown in the figure, I started typing *corection of*. Google correctly guessed that I meant *correction of* and came up with a number of suggestions starting with *correction of*.

I completed the phrase *corection of misspelings* with two misspelled words (Figure 1-38, page 57). Google discovered both misspellings and suggested the correct spelling *correction of misspelling.*

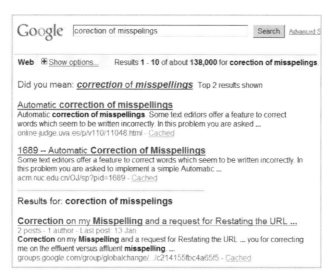

Figure 1-38   Google suggests the correct spelling

Google has observed that some users overlook the suggestion for the correct spelling. For this reason, Google now routinely displays the first couple of results found with the correct spelling on the top of the results list. Below these results, Google claims to display the results found by searching for the incorrectly spelled words (Figure 1-38).

However, when I went through the first 10 results, I only found one page with one of the two misspellings. When I checked the cached version of the pages, it said that the two misspelled words (*corection* and *misspel-ing*) only occurred in the links to the page in question. Furthermore, when I made a search for the correctly spelled words (*correction of misspellings*) Google displayed about the same number of results as for the incorrect spelling. Most likely, Google displayed all the pages where the words were spelled correctly - despite Google's claim to the opposite. I confirmed this by searching for *+corection of +misspelings*. For this query, Google only found one result (not shown) - compared with the 138,000 it claimed to find (see Statistics Bar in Figure 1-38).

Google actually admits that it includes words similar to the misspelled ones. When you go to the bottom of the second results page, you are informed that the results include words similar to the words in your search (Figure 1-39, page 58).

You then get a link to the pages, on which the words should be spelled exactly as you have typed them (Figure 1-39). However, it turns out that

Google only enforces the search engine to look for pages with the first misspelling *corection* - by putting a plus before the word (Figure 1-40).

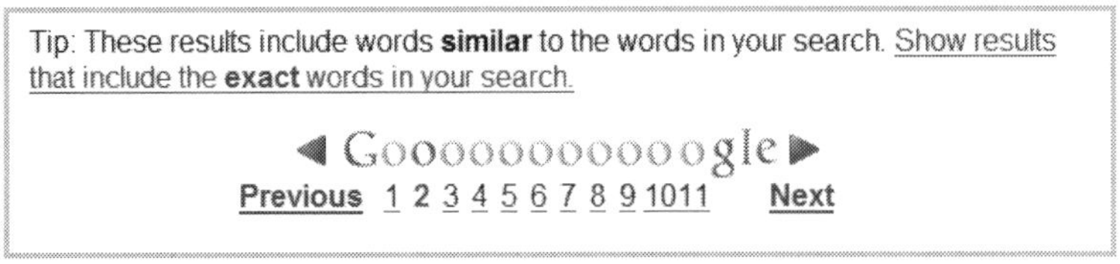

Tip: These results include words **similar** to the words in your search. Show results that include the **exact** words in your search.

◀ Goooooooooo gle ▶
Previous 1 2 3 4 5 6 7 8 9 10 11   **Next**

Figure 1-39   Google displayed results including similar words

To search for the words as spelled, Google should either put a + sign in front of each of the misspelled words or enclose the phrase within quotation marks.

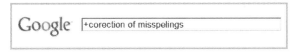

Figure 1-40   Google searches for pages with one of the misspellings

Google in general makes an excellent job in correction of misspellings. As the example above shows, you should, however, be aware that Google "overlooks" some misspellings, and that it may display results with the correct spellings despite claiming displaying results with the incorrect spelling. Also, remember that you can always enforce Google to look for pages with the word spelled exactly as you want - just by putting a plus (+) before the word.

Summing Up

In this chapter, you have got a thorough introduction to Google Web Search. Among other things, you have learned how to:

- Load the US Google search homepage
- Use the Google search box
- Read the results page
- Write specific queries with four or more keywords to increase your chance of getting relevant results
- Search for exact phrases to increase the number of relevant results
- Use natural language phrases to increase the chance of getting the relevant results to the top of the results list

- Benefit from Google Suggest, also known as Query suggestions, when writing queries
- Use the tilde (~) operator to enforce Google to search for synonyms
- Use the OR operator to expand your search
- Use the OR operator to control, which synonyms and word forms to include in the search
- Use the wildcard operator (*) to get Google to suggest missing words

On the way, you have also got the first insight into how Google Web Search really works. Below, we briefly sum up the more important lessons learned.

Improve the Content Score to Get Relevant Results

Most importantly, you have learned that Google ranks results based on an overall score for each Web page. The overall score is calculated from the specific content score and the general popularity score for each Web page. You can't do anything about the popularity score, but you can improve the content score substantially by writing effective queries in natural language with many keywords and meaningful phrases. By increasing the content score, you push the relevant results to the top of the search results list.

Get Inspiration from Google Suggest

You saw that Google Suggest, also known as Query suggestions, is a powerful tool in itself. Furthermore, it is also a great inspiration for learning how to write queries based on popular search terms. You learned that you should be careful not to overlook more specific and relevant search terms by jumping to suggested queries or Web pages too early.

Get More Control over Your Search

Google comes with many effective and valuable tools to assist you in your search such as:

- Automatic inclusion of synonyms to expand your search
- Automatic inclusion of closely related word forms
- Automatic inclusion of meaningful stopwords
- Automatic correction of misspellings

While these tools are in general useful and effective, you may now and then need to put them out of action to get more control over your search.

By using the OR operator, you can enforce Google to include the specific synonyms and word forms you want. However, use of the OR operator doesn't prevent Google from including additional synonyms and word forms.

In contrast, you can completely prevent Google from including synonyms, word forms, and stopwords you don't want. You simply place a minus sign (-) in front of any word, Google must leave out.

In summary, you can usually rely on the Google to handle your search – if you start out with a good query. Google in most cases does an excellent job, but as you have already seen there are a number of situations, where you need to take control to get the most relevant results to the top of the results list. In this chapter, you have seen that the OR and plus and minus operators make it possible for you to exert considerable control over Google's search. In the remaining chapters, you'll learn about other options and tools for refining and controlling your search.

Chapter 2

Working with the Results Page

In this chapter, you first learn how to read the results page and how to get as much information out of it as possible. You then learn how to use the results page as a starting point for refining your search, so you can find the results of the highest relevance to your topic.

Note that Google uses the term results page for a page displaying links to the Web pages that contain information of relevance to your query. Usually, the search results will be distributed over several pages. As standard, each results page displays 10 results. Under Search settings (Global preferences), you can select 10, 20, 30, 50, or 100 results to be displayed per results page (see page 180).

Reading the Results Page

Figure 2-1 (page 62) shows a results page. If you have used Google Web Search before, you may find this results page to be a little unusual, because I have set the number of results to be shown to 1, so you only see one search result. This way you can easily see both the top and the bottom of the results page in the figure. When you start working with the results page, you may benefit from setting the number of results to less than the 10, so you can constantly see its top and bottom and the many options Google offers for modifying your initial search. On page 180, you can read how to set the number of pages to be shown to be less than 10.

To make it easier for you to follow the description of the results page, each major feature has been labeled with circled letters from A to P. The letter J has been skipped to avoid any confusion with the letter I. The first letters in the alphabet have been used for the elements that you presumably use most often. The description of the figure on the following pages follows the letter in alphabetic order. The letters are not part of the results page as you see it on the screen. They have only been inserted here for easy reference. To make it easier for you to follow the description, the details of the figure are shown again as individual figures in close relation to the description of each feature.

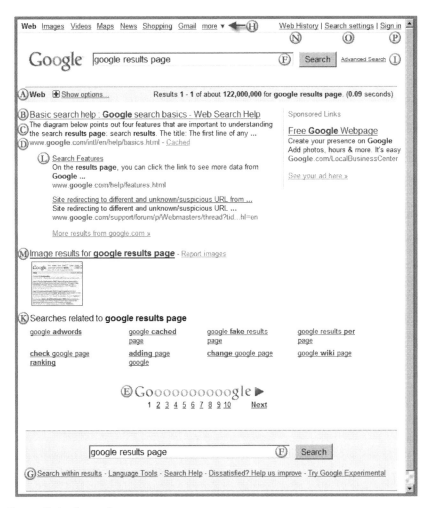

Figure 2-1   A results page

The Statistics Bar

The bar labeled A in the top of Figure 2-1 is often called the Statistics bar. It gives you some statistics and other information about your search. It also contains the Show options button, which gives you access to the Options panel (see below).

First, you are informed about the type of results you are looking at (Figure 2-2, A, page63). In the left corner, you see the word Web. It means that the results page shows all Web results related to your keywords. By use of the Navigation bar at the top of the page (Figure 2-1, H), you can choose to see only a subgroup of results, for example Images. If you select Images, the Statistics Bar displays the word Images in the left corner. You can read more about the Navigation bar on page 79.

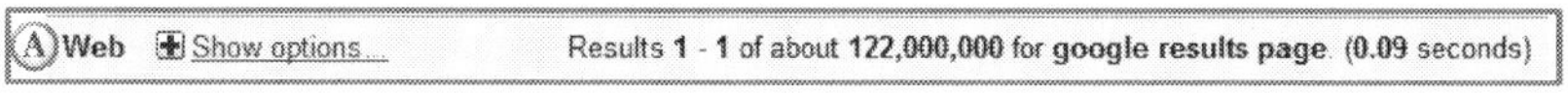

Figure 2-2   The Statistics Bar

Show Options
The next part of the Statistics Bar is a button called Show options (Figure 2-2). Among other things, it gives you access to restrict your search to different types of results and different time periods. In addition, you can use the Options panel to expand or otherwise modify your search. The Options panel is also known as the Options menu. The Options panel is described on page 83 to 103.

Number of Results
The Statistics Bar reminds you how many result you see on each page. In the example in the figure, it is only one. The standard is as mentioned 10 results per page. You are also told how many results Google found. For the same query, the number may vary somewhat from search to search.

Although many searches lead to an impressively high number of results pages, remember that you can see at most 1,000 results (page 27). Also, remember that the important thing is to find the most relevant pages – not the highest number of pages.

Search Query Reminder
The Statistics Bar reminds you what you search phrase is, here *google results page*.

Why are some keywords followed by [definition]?
Until recently, the search query reminder on the Statistics Bar would regularly show some keywords in blue (and the remaining keywords in black). You could click on the blue ones to get a definition. Google seems to have changed this feature. Today, all keywords are in black, but now and then you'll find a keyword in black followed by [definition] in blue. When you click on [definition], you get to Google's English dictionary, where you can read about the different meanings of the word. Google seems to use this feature only for words with several different meanings such as bank, bass, and crane. In academic language, such words are known as polysemes.

Reading a Search Result

The search results matching your query are listed on the results page in a ranked order. The ranking is based both on the relevance to your specific query and on the general popularity of the page among all Web users (see How Google Ranks Search Results, page 29). Each search result shows at least the page title (Figure 2-3, B) the snippet (Figure 2-3, C), and the page's URL address (Figure 2-3, D).

Figure 2-3   A search result with page title (B), snippet (C), and URL (D)

The Page Title

The line labeled B (Figure 2-3) is the title of one of the Web pages, which Google found. In this case, it is number one – the result considered by Google to be the result best matching your search query. The page title is a hyperlink. When you click on it, you are taken to the Web page. Google shows the page title as it is written by the Web site owner.

The Snippet

To make it easier for you to decide, if a search result is of interest, Google gives you a short summary of the Web page just below the result line itself. This is called a snippet (Figure 2-3, C). Google tries to present the information it considers most relevant to your query in the snippet. To do this, Google utilizes all available information – the title, the Web page text, the URL, and the meta-description. The meta-description is written by the Web page author. It describes the Web page content. The meta-description is not displayed by the Web browser. Google may include information from the meta-description in the snippet, if the meta-description is considered relevant to the Web page. As standard, Google shows only about 20 words in the snippet. You can use the Page preview option on the Options panel (page 102) to see more of the snippet text.

The snippet sometimes contain more information
Google is continuously working to improve the information in the snippet. They have introduced a feature called Rich snippet. A Rich snippet may contain ratings of products and services, contact information for a business, and so on. You don't need to do anything

to view this information. If the Web page contains such information, the search result will automatically display it.

The URL Address
All results listed on the results page shows the URL address beneath the snippet (Figure 2-3, D, page 64). Just to the right of the URL address, you often find two links called *cached* and *similar*.

The Cached Link
The link *cached* takes you to a cached version of the results page (Figure 2-4). The cached version is the version of the Web page Google stores on its server. It shows the page exactly as it looked, when the Googlebot (page 31) last visited the page.

You may benefit from visiting the cached page in the following situations:

- The current page is not available.
- You don't find the information you expect on the current page.
- You want to see each search term highlighted in different colors.

Figure 2-4   The Cached Version of a Web page

When you visit a cached page, you are informed that you are looking at a cached version – not the current page. Google also tells you when the page was last visited. More importantly, the search terms on the page are highlighted in different colors. This makes it easy to see, where a specific keyword is mentioned on the page.

You are also informed, if one (or more) of your keywords is not found on the page (title, text, or URL), but only on another page linking to the page. In the example shown in Figure 2-4 (page 65), it is probably the most important information you get. The query was here *google results page cached version*. The term *cached*, which was seen as the most important keyword in this query, is not at all found on the Web page – but only in links to the page.

The Similar Link
The similar link takes you to pages, which may contain information similar to the page you are visiting. It sometimes leads you to further information of relevance to your search. However, unfortunately this is not always the case. You shouldn't rely on this feature as a substitute for your own refinement of your search. The *similar* feature is discussed on page 136 and page 162.

The Plus Box
Sometimes, you may find a so-called Plus box just below the snippet. There is no Plus box in Figure 2-1 (page 62). Figure 2-5 shows a Plus box from an earlier screenshot. The Plus box is used for various purposes. Among other things, you may find more results from the same site, for example, a link to a map showing the company's address.

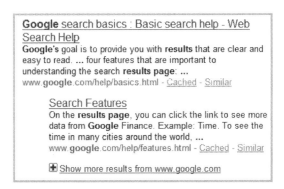

Figure 2-5   A Plus box

The Google Page Bar
At the bottom of the results page, you find a bar (Figure 2-1, E, and Figure 2-6, E, page 63). The bar has no official name, but we here call it the

Google Page bar or just the Page bar. It consists of the name Google spelled (initially) with 10 O's. Under each O, you find a number from 1 to 10. Google as standard shows 10 results per page.

Figure 2-6   The Google Page bar

You use the Google Page Bar to browse through the results pages. To see the next page of results, just click **Next**. You may also click on one of the numbers to get to a specific set of results. If you, for example, want to see the last results, you may click on **10**. In the standard setup, you then get to results number 91 – 100. If Google knows more results than can be displayed on 10 pages, the Page Bar expands. It may give you direct access to up to 20 results pages. The name Google then contains 20 O's (Figure 2-7).

Figure 2-7   An expanded Page bar

When the bar expands, you get access to an arrow named Previous. You can now easily browse forwards and backwards between the results pages. You may click on one of the O's instead of the number below the O to get to a results page.

The Google Page Bar is useful for browsing through results pages with the standard setting displaying 10 pages per results page. However, you may benefit from setting a higher number of results to be displayed per results page, for example 20. If you want to view more than 10 results per page for all your searches, you should change the setting under Search settings (Global preferences, page 180). If you want to change the number of results displayed per page for your current search only, you can change it on the Advanced Search form (page 112).

In general, you should skim a minimum of 20 results for each query. Much valuable information is often found below the top 10 results.

Using the Results Page

Your search doesn't always end when you land on the first results page. Often, you may benefit from seeing the first results page as the starting point for refining your search.

From the first results, you often get a good idea how to make a more precise search. You get a better understanding of your topic by skimming the first few results pages. You learn what words and terms people use in relation to your topic. Usually, you can make a much more qualified query than when you started out.

To improve your query, you may want start from the beginning again. However, Google offers you a number of ways to continue your search from the results page. This is often more effective than starting from scratch again.

The Results Page Search Boxes

The results page contains two identical search boxes – one on the top of the page and another at the bottom (Figure 2-1, F, page 62). The search box at the bottom is shown in Figure 2-8, F.

Figure 2-8   Search box at the bottom of a results page

You may use the search box to modify your query. You can, for example, add more keywords to focus your search. Adding one or two qualifying keywords is often all that is needed to get results that are more relevant.

Note that you may use both simple search operators (such as *OR*) and advanced operators (such as the *intitle:keyword*) directly in the search box. This way, you can make highly focused searches from the search box on the results page when you have seen the first results. You can read about the operators and their use in Chapter 4.

Tools for Modifying Your Search

Just beneath the search box at the bottom of the page, you find links to some additional tools to modify your search and to help you better understand your search results (Figure 2-8, G, page 68). They are:

- Search within results
- Language Tools
- Search Help

At the bottom of the results page, you also find a link to a Google page where you can express any dissatisfaction with the search results. The link is (Figure 2-8, G):

- Dissatisfied? Help us to improve

Recently, Google added an extra link, which takes you to a page inviting you to join one of their experimental programs. The link is called Try Google Experimental (Figure 2-8 G).

Search within Results

When you click Search within Results, you get access to a search box (Figure 2-9), in which you can modify your original search. You may, for example, enter additional keywords.

Figure 2-9   Search within results

In relation to the new keywords, you add, you can use most of the simple and advanced operators. For example, you may use the advanced operator *intitle* (page 152) to specify that one of the original keywords must occur in the title of the Web pages displayed. You can even combine simple and advanced operators as shown in Figure 2-10, page 70. You can read about operators in Chapter 4.

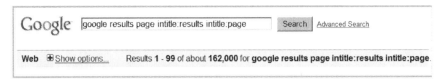

Figure 2-10   Focusing of a search by use of operators

However, you can't go back and change anything within the original query when you use Search within results. As the name point to, you can only focus the search within the results you already have got. You may, therefore, prefer to use the search box at the top or bottom of the re- sults page. By using one of these search boxes, you can modify your initial search query without any restrictions. You may, for example, mod- ify or delete one or more of your original keywords. Use of a simple search box gives you more flexibility.

Language Tools

The link Language Tools (Figure 2-1, G, page 62, and Figure 2-8, G, page 68) gives you access to five language services. The first four are shown in Figure 2-11, page 71. The fifth tool is shown in Figure 2-21, page 78.

The five services are:

- Translated search (Figure 2-11, A)
- Translate text (Figure 2-11, B)
- Translate a web page (Figure 2-11, C)
- Use the Google Interface in Your Language (Figure 2-11, D)
- Visit Google's site in Your Local Domain (Figure 2-21)

Translated Search

You may benefit from searching for information in more than one lan- guage. The more specialized your information need is, the more you benefit from searching within more languages. However, only few people really master more than one or two foreign languages. Here Translated search offers highly valuable help.

By use of Translated search (Figure 2-11, A), you can enter your query in your own languages. Google then translates your query into one or more other languages, searches the Web in these languages, finds the relevant results, and translates the results back into your own language.

70

Figure 2-11   Language Tools

Google has not made known, which factors, they use for deciding which languages to include. However, you can decide to leave out one or more of the languages chosen by Google. You can also add a language. This way you may control which languages Translated search includes. Alternatively, you can select the languages you want to include from the beginning. Below, you learn how to use both options.

How to use Translated Search

1. Enter your query into the search box (Figure 2-12, A, page 72). In the example shown in the figure, the query is *google language tools*.

2. Choose how you want to select the languages to be included in your search (Figure 2-12, B). You can choose between **Automatically selected languages** or **Specific languages**. If you choose Specific languages, you must select the language or languages to be included (see below and Figure 2-13, page 72).

71

3. Select the language, in which you have written you query. It is called My language (Figure 2-12, C). In the example here, it is English. To select another language, click on the arrow and select the language. You can currently choose between 42 different languages including English.
4. Click **Translate and Search** (Figure 2-12, D).

Figure 2-12   Translated search

Figure 2-13   Translated search for specific languages

How to Select the Languages to be Included in the Search
1. Click **Specific Languages** (Figure 2-12, B).

2. Click the check boxes for the languages you want to include. In the example in Figure 2-13, page 72, I have selected Danish, French, and German.

How to read the Results from Translated Search

Let us assume that we made a Translated search for the query *google language tools* as shown in Figure 2-12. In this example, we let Translated search select the languages to be included. The result is shown in Figure 2-14.

The Translated search results page gives you several options to improve and expand the translated search. Below, we go through the Translated search results page. First we take a look on the overall structure of the Translated search results page. The results page can be divided into three parts (Figure 2-14):

- At the top, you find the Statistics Bar (Figure 2-14, A)
- In the middle, you get a text box with information about the languages included in the Translated search (Figure 2-14, B), the translated query for each language (Figure 2-14, C), and the number of search results for each language (Figure 2-14, D).
- In the lower half of the page (Figure 2-14, G and H), you see the search results for all selected languages together – ranked by relevance to your query and general popularity.

Figure 2-14   Translated search results page

Statistics Bar

In the Statistics Bar, you are informed that the results displayed are Web results from a Translated search (Figure 2-14, A, page 73). "Web" here means that all types of results (text, images, and so on) are displayed (see also page 62).

The number of results shown in black on the Statistics Bar is the total number of results found by all the translated searches. This number doesn't include the number of results in your own language, here English. To see these results, you have to click on **Web** in the left corner of the Statistics Bar (Figure 2-14, A).

Translated results

Below the Statistics Bar, you find a box showing the languages included by Translated search (Figure 2-14, B), the translated query for each language (Figure 2-14, C), and the number of results in each language (Figure 2-14, D).

You can exclude one or more of the languages automatically included by Translated search. To exclude a language, click on the **check box** (Figure 2-14, B) to the right of the language. In the example shown in Figure 2-15, I am about to exclude Spanish by clicking the check box. The content of the box is the updated, now displaying only the data for the remaining languages (not shown).

You can also ask Translated search to include one additional language. Click on **Add Language** (Figure 2-14, E). Select the additional language to be included. You can only include one additional language this way.

Translated results for **google language tools** - My language: English ▼

Language	Translated query		
Spanish ☒	**herramientas de idioma de Google** - Edit	3.420.000 results
German ☒	**Google Sprach-Tools** - Edit	3.410.000 results

Figure 2-15   Leaving out a language from translated search

Google also shows the translated query used for each foreign language. If you know the foreign language well and think that another translation could be better, you can edit the translated query. Click on **edit** to the right of the translated query (Figure 2-14, C), and modify the translated query or write a new. In the example shown in Figure 2-14, it might be worth trying the translated query *google sprachwerkzeuge* (Figure 2-16, page 75). *Sprachwerkzeuge* is the "correct" German translation of *lan-*

guage tools. However, when I used this translation, Translated search only found about 90,000 results in comparison with the 3,670,000 results found with *Google Sprach-Tools*. This shows that the mixed German-English word *Sprach-tools* is used much more on Web pages in German than the German word *Sprachwerkzeuge*. However, as always, remember that it is the relevance of the results that counts - not the amount. Therefore, it may be worth skimming also the first 20 results found by use of the "correct" German translation.

Figure 2-16   Editing of the translated query

You can view the results for each language separately. To do this, click in the number of results for the language in question (Figure 2-14, D, page 73).

Finally, you may change the primary language. In Figure 2-14, F, the primary language is English. You can select one of the other 41 languages. However, here it begins to become somewhat complicated. If you, for example, select German in the example shown in Figure 2-14, the Translated search is carried out for the query *google language tools* in English and Turkish (Figure 2-17). If you want to select a new primary language, I suggest you start over again and write the query in the new primary language.

Figure 2-17   Selection of a new Primary language, here German

Search results
Below the text box with the information about the Translated search, you find the search results for the selected languages. As shown in Figure 2-14, G and H, results from different languages are mixed between each other.

Translate Text

When you use Translated search, Google translates your query to the foreign languages selected. The Web pages found in the foreign languages are then automatically translated back into your language. You don't need to translate any part of the text yourself. However, you may now and then want to translate a limited part of a Web page, or a text, you have found elsewhere. In this situation, you can use the Translate text tool (Figure 2-11, B, page 71). Copy and paste the text into the box in the Translate text tool and click **Translate** (Figure 2-18). Remember to select the right languages. If the text is in another language than the one you select to translate it from, the translation doesn't work.

Figure 2-18   Translate text tool

Translate a Web page

You may also want to translate a complete Web page. To do this, just copy the Web address from the address bar in your browser and paste it into the address box in the Translate a web page tool (Figure 2-11, C, page 71, and Figure 2-19).

Figure 2-19   Translate a web page tool

Note that the address box in the Translate a Web page tool already contains *http://*. Be careful not to include any part of *http://* in the Web address, when you copy the address from the browser's address bar. If you, for example, happen to copy an extra slash (/), the tool will not recognize the address as a valid URL address and the page will not be translated.

Use the Google Interface in Your language
The language, in which the menus, help text, and so on are written, is called the interface language. You can use Language tools (Figure 2-11 D, page 71) to change the interface language, so you get the Google search page in another language.

The Google search page is currently available in 129 languages. Of these, five languages: 1) Bork Bork Bork, 2) Elmer Fudd, 3) Hacker, 4) Klingon, and 5) Pirate, are artificial languages. You can't really use these languages, when you search. They are just there for fun.

You can change the interface language by clicking on the language you want as interface language. The interface languages are shown in five columns. The first three rows of the table are shown in Figure 2-20.

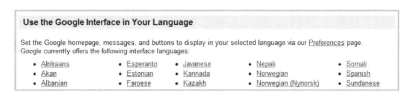

Figure 2-20   Interface languages

When you change the interface language on the Language Tools page, it only applies to your current search session. If you want to change the interface language permanently, change it under Search settings (Global preferences, page 174).

Visit Google's Site in Your Local Domain
Besides the US main Google search page, there exist many local Google search pages. The local search pages are also known as local domain search pages. Currently, there are close to 180 local search pages. The idea behind the local search pages is that they should be used for searches within a geographical area. As an example, the Google search page www.google.de is meant for searches on pages located in Germany.

The local search pages are shown in a table-like menu with five columns. Figure 2-21 (page 78) shows the first two rows. You may visit a local page by clicking on the name of the local page you want to use.

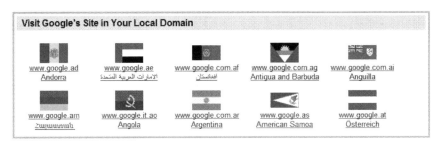

Figure 2-21 Google's Local Domain Sites

Note that selection of a local domain search page not necessarily results in change of the interface language. Initially, the interface language may remain your primary language. When you land on the local search page, you get the possibility to change to the local interface language, if Google has not already done this for you. However, you probably want to keep your primary language as interface language, unless you know the local language well.

Benefit of local search page when you live outside the region

When you use a local search page instead of Google's main US search page, pages from the location chosen are likely to get a higher ranking than pages from outside the region. If you, for example, are located in the US and select the Danish search page, Web pages from Denmark tend to get higher rank than pages from other regions. The practical importance of this depends on your search topic. In general, it seems to be most useful when you search for shops, services, and other commercial activities.

Google has recently (end of February 2010) introduced an option, Nearby, which should further improve your chance of getting results of local interest on top of the results lists (see page 94).

Benefit of local pages when you live in the region

If you live outside US, you most likely want to use your local search page for your everyday searches. If you are primarily interested in local information, you should use the local search page and also set the search language to the local language (see page 175). Usually, you don't have to bother about this. From your IP-address, Google knows where you are located and usually selects your local search page and search Language for you (see also page 5 and page 94).

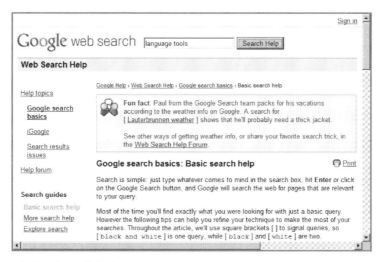

Figure 2-22   Search help

Search Help

The last of the tools found at the bottom of the bottom of the results page (Figure 2-1, G, page 62, and Figure 2-8, G, page 68), is the Search help. Click on this link, if you need help to your Google Web Search.

On the Search help page (Figure 2-22), you find some general advices about how Google search works and how to optimize your search. Note the menu to the left. It contains links to many useful pages. Maybe even more importantly, you find the Google web search help search box on the top of the page. Enter a search phrase here to get help about your search question or problem.

Google Navigation Bar

You find the Google navigation bar on the top-left of the results page (Figure 2-1 H, Figure 2-23, and Figure 2-24, page 80). You usually search the whole Web when you start a search. You can use the Google navigation bar to restrict your search to images, videos, maps, news, shopping, and so on. The Google navigation bar also gives you access to other Google services and tools such as Gmail. Click **more** to get access to even more tools.

Figure 2-23   Google Navigation bar – from www.google.dk

Note that the Google navigation bar may differ from one country to another - even when the interface language is set to English. Compare Figure 2-23, page 79, and Figure 2-24.

Figure 2-24   Google Navigation bar – from www.google.co.uk

Advanced Search

To the right of the Search button on the top of the results page (Figure 2-1, I, page 62, and Figure 2-25, I) you find a link to Advanced Search. It takes you to the Advanced Search form. You can read in Chapter 3, how to use the Advanced Search form.

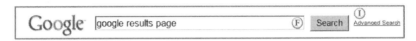

Figure 2-25   Link to Advanced Search

Related Searches

At the bottom of the results page, Google usually suggests a number of related searches (Figure 2-1, K, page 62, and Figure 2-26, K).

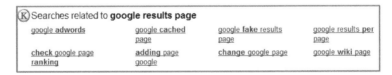

Figure 2-26   Related searches

This feature was introduced in March 2009. Google describes the improvement this way: *"Starting today, we're deploying a new technology that can better understand associations and concepts related to your search, and one of its first applications lets us offer you even more useful related searches (the terms found at the bottom, and sometimes at the top, of the search results page)"*.

The usefulness of the related searches depends on your search query. If you have searched for information for a general topic, you may get only vaguely relevant related searches. As an example, if your query is *google results page* as in the example in Figure 2-26 (page 80), it may not be easy for Google to determine how a related search should look. The search query is not very specific. It contains three general keywords. This makes it difficult for Google to come up with highly relevant related searches. If you wanted to learn how to read and use the results page, you wouldn't find much relevant stuff in the related searches shown in Figure 2-26. In contrast, you may find highly relevant related searches, if your search is within a narrow scientific or technical field. The only way you can find out, if the suggested related searches are relevant to your topic, is by visiting the pages.

Indented Results

An indented result is as the name clear states a result, which is indented in relation to the previous result on the results list (Figure 2-1, L, page 62). If Google Web Search finds more than one result at the same or closely similar URL addresses, Google may show the second and third result as intended results as shown in Figure 2-1, L. If there are more than two related results, Google displays a link to the remaining results. In Figure 2-1, L, the link is *More results from google.com >*.

Image Results

Besides information in text form, the Web contains many other types of information, for example, images and videos. Web page consisting solely or mainly of an image may, therefore, now and then pop up as a search result (Figure 2-1, M, page 62). To find out, if there is more information on the Web page than the image itself, just click on the image shown.

Web History

Web history (Figure 2-27 N, page 82) among other things gives you access to pages you have visited. Use of Web history requires that you have a Google account, and that you are signed in. As we saw on page 22, Google now offers some customization of the search, even if you don't have a Google account. However, if you don't have a Google account, you can't see the Web history. Google's reason for not allowing you to see the Web history is that several users may be using the same PC. If you are not signed in to your account, Google links the Web history to the PC - not to the individual user. This way, Google can use the Web history, which is stored on their servers, to give you personalized suggestions without disclosing what you and others are searching for.

If you want to be able to see your Web search history, you need to set up a Google account. Google search features related to a Google account is beyond the scope of this book and is not discussed further.

Search Settings

Search settings (Figure 2-1, O, page 62, and Figure 2-27, O) is just a link, which takes you to Global preferences. Google preferences is described in Appendix A (starting on page 171).

Figure 2-27   Web History, Search settings and Sign in

Sign in

By clicking the link Sign in (Figure 2-1 P, page 62, and Figure 2-27, P) you get to your Google account. If you don't have a Google account, you can create one. When you have a Google account, you can customize the search page, view and manage your Web activity (history), and get more personalized search results. As stated in the introduction, this book is dedicated to general Web search. Personalization of the search interface and Web search are not discussed.

Figure 2-28   Sponsored links

We have now completed the general discussion of the results page and move on to look on some of the special features.

Sponsored Links

Sponsored links are Google's name for paid advertisements. Based on your search query, Google tries to find the paid advertisements, which are most relevant to your search query. They may appear either above the proper search results or in a separate column to the right of the search results (Figure 2-28, page 82). They are always clearly labeled Sponsored Links. Furthermore, any Sponsored Link above the proper search results is shown on a colored background.

Options Panel

Google calls this feature both the Options panel and the Options menu. We here use the term Options panel.

The Options panel is a major innovation and improvement in Google Web Search. It was introduced in May 2009. At the introduction, Google announced that the Options panel was still under development, and that it would be modified now and then. Actually, the Options panel has undergone numerous changes since its introduction. New features have been added. Others have disappeared for a period just to reappear again later. As an example, the option Time line was missing in a period, but is currently (March 2010) back again. Other options once present such as Most recent results are at present missing and may have gone permanently. The option to search for Nearby results was added end of February 2010.

The Options panel most likely hasn't found its final version yet. Due to the rapid evaluation in the way, we search, and in the development of the Web, it is unlikely that there will ever be a "final version". The frequent changes have necessitated rewriting of this section of the book several times. The description you are reading now is based on the situation March 1, 2010. Rumors say that Google soon may introduce a new results page, in which the Options panel is displayed as soon as you have done the search. Today, you have to click the Show options button to see the Options panel (see Figure 2-1 A, page 62, and Figure 2-29, A, page 84).

Options Panel Overview

In this section, you first learn how to access the Options panel. We then go through the functions of the Options panel and the various options you get for restricting, expanding, and viewing your search results.

Opening the Options Panel

Click the Show options button on the Statistics Bar (Figure 2-29).

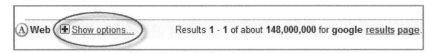

Figure 2-29   The Show options button on the Statistics bar

When you click the Show options button, the Options panel becomes visible on the results page to the left of the results (Figure 2-30).

Figure 2-30   The Options panel – as it looked March 1, 2010

The Five Main Categories in the Options Panel

The various search options in the Options panel are grouped into five main categories (Figure 2-30, page 84). Google seems to prefer to call them modes, but the term filters is also used. The five modes apparently have no official name. Here, we use the term modes and give each mode a name to make reference easier. The five modes are:

- Results mode (Figure 2-30, A)
- Time mode (Figure 2-30, B)
- Location mode (Figure 2-30, C)
- View mode (Figure 2-30, D)
- Display mode (Figure 2-30, E)

Below, we first list the options you can choose for each main category (mode). In the sections following this overview, you learn about the use of each option.

Results mode

You use the Results mode to filter and view the results by type (Figure 2-30, A). You can currently choose between the following types of results:

- All results
- Images
- Videos
- News
- Blogs
- Updates
- Books
- Discussions (formerly Forums)

Time mode

You use the Time mode to filter and view the results by time (Figure 2-30, B). You can currently choose between the following time filters:

- Any time
- Latest
- Past 24 hours
- Past week
- Past year
- Specific date range

Location mode

You use Location mode to filter and view results by location (Figure 2-30, C, page 84). You can currently choose between the following location filters:

- All results
- Nearby

View mode

The View mode category contains some mixed tools. You primarily use the View mode tools to expand your search. You can currently choose between the following options (Figure 2-30, D):

- Standard view
- Related searches
- Wonder wheel
- Timeline

Presentation mode

The Presentation mode category contains some mixed tools. You use the Presentation mode to restrict or expand your search depending on your choice of options. You can currently choose between the following presentation modes (Figure 2-30, E):

- Standard results
- Images from the page
- Fewer shopping sites
- More shopping sites
- Page previews
- Translated search

The options within each of the five main modes are described in the following sections.

Filter Results by Type

To filter the results by type, click one of the options **Images**, **Videos**, **News**, **Blogs**, **Updates**, **Books**, or **Discussions** (Figure 2-31, page 87). Discussions were until early February 2010 called Forums. The standard is All Results. When you have selected a subgroup of the results, for example, Images, you can always go back to see all results again by clicking **All results**. Your selection is shown in bold (Figure 2-32, page 87).

The Statistics Bar also tells you where you are. This makes it easy for you to navigate from one type of results to another.

When you select an option, you often get access to new options. When you, for example, select Images, you get access to filter the images by size, type, and color (not shown).

Figure 2-31   Results mode

Figure 2-32   Results mode with images selected

Images
When you click **Images**, you get to the images related to your search. As mentioned, you can filter the images results further. The options are size, type, and color. Discussion of Google image search is outside the scoop of this book.

Videos
When you click **Videos**, you get to the videos related to your search. You are offered many options to restrict or sort the video results. The options currently are: duration (0-4 min.; 4 – 20 min., 20+ min.), time (past hour, past 24 hours, past week, past year, specific data range), quality (all, high), type (all, closed caption), and source (youtube.com, google.com, and so on). The sources of the videos you can view depend on your search terms. Discussion of Google video search is outside the scoop of this book.

News

The News option gives you, as the name clearly state, access to News related to your query. It may be seen as a shortcut to Google News. According to Google, the News option in the Options panel limits the results to Google News index. You should, therefore, find the same results as when you start your search from Google News. However, this is not always the case.

For recent or on-going events, for example, *climate talks*, there is no significant difference in the results found by the two methods. You get essentially the same results when you start from Google Web Search and select the option News, as when you start directly from Google News. However, for topics, which are not so hot or popular, you may find different results by the two methods.

If you are doing a general Web information search, as we are focusing on in this book, you can use the News option to get an idea about the recent and current activities within your topic. However, Google News usually gives you a broader picture. You may want to try out both methods to be sure to find all recent results of relevance.

There are also other differences between starting a search from Google Web Search and from Google News. Among other things, the query suggestions, you get from Google Suggest may differ, in particular for current topics.

Blogs

Blog is an abbreviation for Web log. It is a web site that regularly publishes news or comments on a topic. Some, but not all blog sites (blogs), allow comments by the readers, whereas blogs seldom functions as proper discussion forums. The boundary to forums (today named Discussions by Google) is, however, becoming increasingly blurred. The material found on blogs often express personal points of view. You may find much valuable information on many blogs. Note in this context that some companies, including Google, use blogs as official information channels. The Official Google Blog (http://googleblog.blogspot.com) is one of the best place to learn about new Google ideas, programs, search features, and so on.

When you click **Blogs**, you get access to a detailed time filtering (Figure 2-33, page 89).

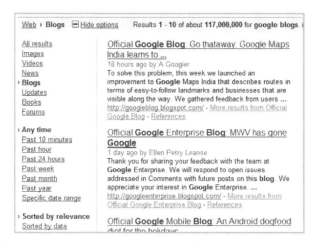

Figure 2-33   Blog documents can be sorted by time or relevance

Updates

Early December 2009 Google went into a partnership with Facebook, MySpace, Twitter, FriendFeed, Jaiku, and Identi.ca. This means that you can now get updates from these services in real-time (Figure 2-34). These services have in common that they are all part of the Web social networking, also known as Web 2.0. People use these services to tell about themselves, make friends, blogging, and so on. Updates are great for following what people are interested in here and now.

Figure 2-34   Updates shows the latest news from Web 2.0 services

When you select Updates, the results from the news feeders mentioned above is continuously updated in real-time. The newest results available are being added to the top of the results list as you watch. To get the updates in real-time, select the option **Latest** (see arrow A in Figure 2-

34, page 89). The option Latest is the standard setting. If you are watching a very hot topic, you may find that the news is coming in too fast. You can then break the news feed by clicking **Pause** at the top of the list (Figure 2-34, B).

Books

When you click **Books**, Google displays only the results found in the Google Books index (Figure 2-35). Google has started an ambitious project of making all books in the World available in digital form from Google's servers. The project has not been welcomed by all. Nonetheless, thousands of interesting books are today available on Google Books and the number is rapidly increasing.

Figure 2-35   Restriction of search results to Books

Note that you get some interesting new filtering options when you have clicked Books. First, you can choose between three different views (Any view, Preview and full view, and Full view (Figure 2-35). Second, you can get different types of documents displayed (Any document, Books, and Magazines). The two filters may be combined. For example, you can restrict your search to Preview and full view, and Magazines.

You can get to Google Books directly at http://books.google.com. Google Books is a program in itself. Discussion of the many interesting features of Google Books is outside the scope of this book. However, you should know that you sometimes may find information in Google Books, which is not easily found by a general Web search. The information in books and magazines in general has been edited and is usually reliable, but not always fully up-to-date.

Discussions (Forums)

Forums are discussion groups. Early February 2010 Google renamed Forums to Discussions. In general, they differ from blogs by being written by several people engaged in a discussion of a topic. Often, they are restricted to discussion of a specific issue. The discussion may be moderated by a person, who has or has been given some authority. In general, forums are more formal than blogs. As stated above, the boundary between blogs and forums is blurred. You may want to visit both blogs and forums to see, if you can find a blog or forum discussing your topic.

Figure 2-36   Restricting of the search results to Discussions (Forums)

In general, you can join a forum yourself and ask questions. Forums are often great for getting answers to very specific questions. There are many forums devoted to discussion of Google search issues.

When you select the option Discussions, you get access to a number of additional sorting options (Figure 2-36). As for some of the other options, you can sort results by relevance or date (Figure 2-36, A). You can choose to read proper Forums or Q&As (Figure 2-36, B). Google has kept the name Forums for a part of the Discussions option. Finally, you can filter the results by length (Figure 2-36, C). You can choose between Any, Short, Medium, and Long.

Filter Results by Time

You have just learned how to filter results by type. When you have filtered the results by type, you often get the option to filter them further by a second criterion. You can filter most result types by time. Of the eight results types shown in Figure 2-31, page 87, you can filter five types by time: All results, Video, News, Blogs, and Updates.

The time filters are a little different for the various result types. For most of the result types, you get the same time filter options as for All results (see below), but the time length for past periods varies a little. As an example, you can select a past period on only 10 minutes for Blogs, whereas the shortest past period for All results, Videos, News, and Discussions is one hour. For Images and Books, there is no time filter option at all.

The time filter Latest is currently only available for the result types Updates (Figure 2-34, page 89) and All results (Figure 2-37). When you select Latest, the results are updated continuously in real-time. You can break the continuous update by clicking **Pause** on the top of the results list (Figure 2-34, B).

Figure 2-37   Filtering of All results by time Latest

Time Filter Options for All Results

For the result type All results, also named Web results (Figure 2-37, page 92), you get six options for filtering the results by time:

- Any time (no filtering – the standard setting)
- Latest
- Past 24 hours
- Past week
- Past year
- Specific date range

Below, we briefly go through each time filter option for All results.

Any time

This option doesn't sort the results by time at all. Instead, they are sorted by their overall ranking. The overall ranking relevance is determined by the general popularity and specific relevance to your query (see How Google Ranks Search Results on page 29).

Latest

When you select Latest, Google displays the results it finds most relevant and recent. The results are continuously updated.

Past 24 hours, Past week, and Past year

When you select one of these options, Google displays the results from a fixed past period from today. For All results, the options are Past 24 hours, Past week, or Past year.

Specific Date Range

Instead of filtering the results from today and a certain period back in time, you may also limit the results to a specific date range. When you click on **Specific date range**, you get to the Specific date range search box (Figure 2-38).

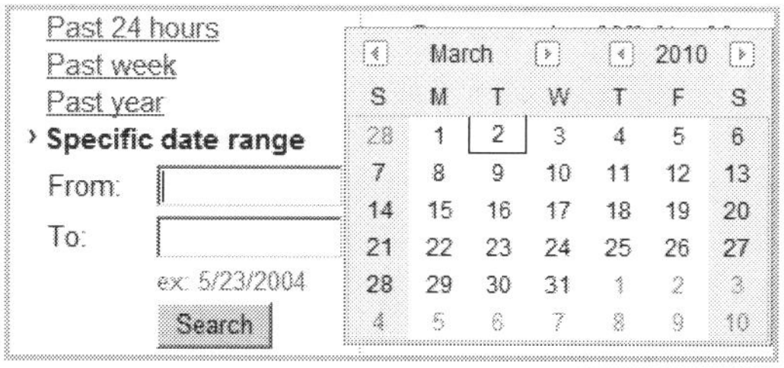

Figure 2-38   Limiting results to a specific date range

Until recently, it could be a challenge to enter the date correctly due to the different date formats in use around the world. Fortunately, Google has recently added a small calendar to the specific date range search option (Figure 2-38, page 93), which pops up when you click specific date range. The calendar makes it easy to enter the date(s) you want. If you want to enter the dates in the date range search boxes, you can read about the date formats in the box below.

About date formats

In the US, you use the format *mm/dd/yyyy*, where mm the month (1 – 12), dd is the date (1 – 31), and yyyy is the year. When you are outside US, Google may still suggest using the US date format, if you have selected English as interface language (page 173) – even if you use your local home page. If you have set the interface language to your own language, you should normally be able to use your country's date format. The date format in most countries outside US is *dd/mm/yyyy*.

I recommend that you try out, how Google interprets the date format on your version of the Google homepage. You can do this by entering a date, which is valid only in one of the two formats, mm/dd/yyyy, or dd/mm/yyyy. You may, for example, try out the date suggested by Google in Figure 2-38 (page 93), 5/23/2004. This is May 23 in 2004. This could not be the date format dd/mm/yyyy, because there are only 12 months. If you enter a non-existing date, Google will inform you about this. This makes it simple to test, if Google wants the date in the US format or in the format used outside US.

In the Timeline date range search box, you'll find a third date format: yyyy/mm/dd (Figure 2-47, page 99).

Filter Results by Location

End of February 2010, Google introduced a new filter. You can now sort search results by Location (Figure 2-30, C, page 84). You can choose between All results (no filtering) or Nearby.

When you choose Nearby, you get several choices for how to define your location (Figure 2-30). As standard, Google displays results for your Default location. If you are signed in to your Google account, your default location is the location you have chosen as your standard (default) location.

94

If you are not signed in, or if you don't have a Google account, Google may attempt to display customized results based on your IP address. This is another example of Google's effort to customize search results, when you don't have or don't use a Google account (see also page 22).

Figure 2-39   Restricting search results to nearby location

When you select Default location, you can further choose between City, Region, and State. These options may be particularly interesting, if you live in US. The option City seems to work well elsewhere, too.

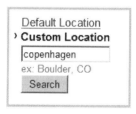

Figure 2-40   Custom location

As an alternative to Default location, you can select Custom location (Figure 2-40). When you click on Custom location, you get access to a box, where you can enter your preferred location. Google may not recognize all locations (cities, regions, and so on). If you enter a location that Google doesn't know, Google will inform you (Figure 2-41).

Figure 2-41   Google didn't recognize the area

Expand Your Search by View Mode

In the View menu (Figure 2-42), you may select four different views.

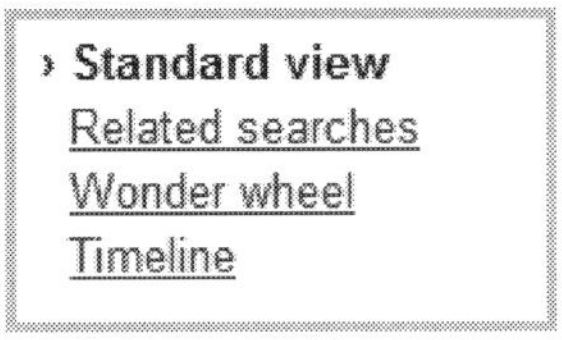

> Standard view
> Related searches
> Wonder wheel
> Timeline

Figure 2-42   The View menu with Standard view selected

Standard View

The standard view is just the way the results are displayed, if you don't select another view.

Related Searches

The Related searches feature is described on page 80. Google sometimes, but not always brings up some related searches at the top or bottom of the results page. If this doesn't happen, you can get Google to display the related searches by clicking on *Related searches* (Figure 2-43).

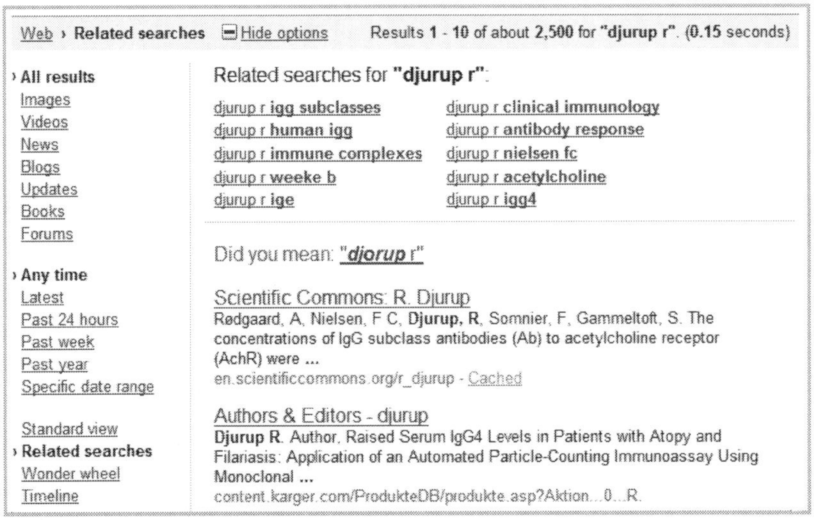

Web › **Related searches** ⊟ Hide options   Results **1 - 10** of about **2,500** for **"djurup r"**. (0.15 seconds)

› **All results**
Images
Videos
News
Blogs
Updates
Books
Forums

› **Any time**
Latest
Past 24 hours
Past week
Past year
Specific date range

Standard view
› **Related searches**
Wonder wheel
Timeline

Related searches for **"djurup r"**:

djurup r **igg subclasses**   djurup r **clinical immunology**
djurup r **human igg**   djurup r **antibody response**
djurup r **immune complexes**   djurup r **nielsen fc**
djurup r **weeke b**   djurup r **acetylcholine**
djurup r **ige**   djurup r **igg4**

Did you mean: *"**djorup** r"*

Scientific Commons: R. Djurup
Rødgaard, A, Nielsen, F C, **Djurup, R**, Somnier, F, Gammeltoft, S. The concentrations of IgG subclass antibodies (Ab) to acetylcholine receptor (AchR) were ...
en.scientificcommons.org/r_djurup - Cached

Authors & Editors - djurup
Djurup R. Author. Raised Serum IgG4 Levels in Patients with Atopy and Filariasis: Application of an Automated Particle-Counting Immunoassay Using Monoclonal ...
content.karger.com/ProdukteDB/produkte.asp?Aktion...0...R.

Figure 2-43   Related searches for "djurup r"

It may be difficult to assess, how accurate, complete, and relevant Google Web Search's related searches are. You can most likely only do this by making some searches where you have a good idea about what related searches could be. As an example, I first searched for my own name as used in citation of scientific papers (*"djurup r"*). I then clicked on **Related searches** (Figure 2-43, page 96).

All related searches displayed by Google in this example are relevant, as they relate to my main research topics back in the 80's. Only one group of related searches was missing. From this example and a small number of similar experiments, Related searches seems to be a valuable tool for expansion of searches – if you are searching for a specific topic. For more general searches, it doesn't always lead you to relevant results (see also page 80).

Wonder wheel

The Wonder wheel view (Figure 2-44) is probably best seen as a graphical display of related searches. Google states: *"The **Wonder wheel** visually presents connections between related searches and your search term as an interactive diagram. Click the different nodes in the diagram to see how searches can branch out"*. However, you don't always get exactly the same results as in the Related searches view (Figure 2-44).

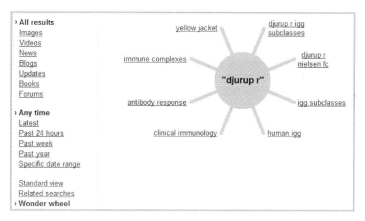

Figure 2-44   Wonder wheel view for "djurup r"

Timeline

Google also offers you to view your search results along a timeline. You may find this useful, if you want to get an overview of how a situation developed over time. You may also want to use this view to learn about major events in a famous person's life.

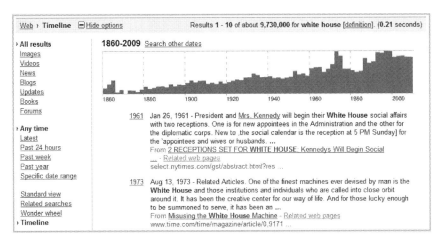

Figure 2-45   Timeline view

You can only select the Timeline view for the result type All results. Figure 2-45 shows the Timeline view for the query *white house*.

At first, Google shows you the time interval, which it considers most relevant – from many years down to one year or maybe even shorter. If you, for example, search for *white house* (Figure 2-45), you find a timeline ranging from 1860 until today. If you search for *bill clinton*, the timeline goes from 1990 until today. The timelines given here are examples. The timeline for any given search may change as more Web pages are added to the Google databases.

From the Timeline view, you can select other dates to be displayed by two different methods. As the first option, you can click **Search other dates** to the right of the data range value(s) shown (Figure 2-46, A).

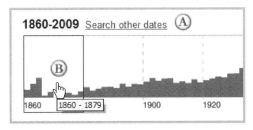

Figure 2-46   Selecting other dates for the Timeline view

When you click **Search other dates**, a search box pops up (Figure 2-47, page 99). Enter your preferred dates (years) into the search boxes.

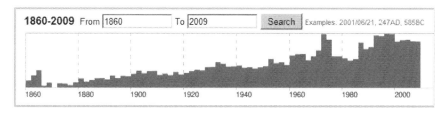

Figure 2-47   Search other dates

Note that the date search boxes accept other date formats than the Specific date range search box (see Specific Date Range, page 93). You can see from the examples shown in grey to the right of search boxes that the valid date formats are yyyy/mm/dd, yyyAC, and yyyBC (Figure 2-47). Most often, you probably want to use the international date format yyyy/mm/dd.

For searches related to early historical events or people, for example, *roman caesars*, you may want to use the date formats BC (Before Christ) or AD (Anno Domini – Latin for Anno Domini – meaning in the year of our Lord).

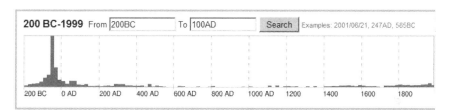

Figure 2-48   Timeline for the query roman caesars *– up to 100AD*

Note, that BC and AD are both written after the year. There is no space between the year number and BC or AD, see example in Figure 2-47. Remember that the higher the BC year the earlier the time. As an example, 300BC comes before 200BC.

As a graphic alternative to typing other dates into the search boxes, you can click on the time range of interest on the timeline itself (Figure 2-46, B, page 98). This way, you may zoom in on shorter time intervals. If you, for example, click on the time interval 1860 – 1879 shown in Figure 2-46, you get to a more detailed view of the Timeline for this period (Figure 2-49, page 100).

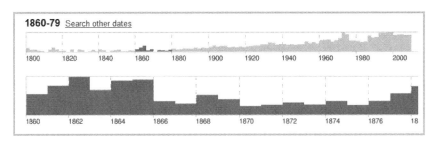

Figure 2-49   Detailed Timeline view – compare with Figure 2-42

To get an even more detailed view, just click in one of the new time in-tervals displayed.

Beware of date range search limitations

Although the recent improvements in the Google search engine's capabilities to search, sort and present results by date in the Time-line are very useful, beware of their limitations. It is not always possible for the search engine to get accurate date information. As an example, Google found results from February 2009 mentioning the disappearance of Air France flight 447 (AF 447). The flight dis-appeared on its flight from Rio de Janeiro to Paris June 1, 2009.

In some situations, the incorrect date reported by Google was due to mix-up of the two date formats: mm/dd/yyyy – used in the U.S. and a few other countries - and dd/mm/yyyy used in Europe and most other areas. For example, some results stated to be from February 7 were actually from July 2.

In other situations, the original document's time stamp was incor-rect. Google reported the time stamp correctly.

Also, note that in many situations an event is not reported when it happens – or shortly after - but first later, when it becomes inter-esting.

Modify Your Search by Display Mode

In the lowest part of the Options panel, you can choose how you want the results displayed (Figure 2-50, page 101).

> ‣ **Standard results**
> Images from the page
> Fewer shopping sites
> More shopping sites
> Page previews
> Translated search

Figure 2-50   The Results display menu

Images from the page

Click **Images from the page**, if you want to see an image related to the search result. One or more images are then shown to the right of the snippet (Figure 2-51). This may give you a clue to whether the results page is actually relevant to your search.

Laptop - Wikipedia, the free encyclopedia
A **laptop** is a personal computer designed for mobile use and small and light enough to sit on one's lap while in use. A **laptop** integrates most of the typical ...
en.wikipedia.org/wiki/**Laptop** - Cached - Similar

Figure 2-51   Display of images from the results page

Fewer shopping sites

Depending on the topic of your search query, many of the results pages may be commercial pages. Commercial pages are here defined as pages where the owner wants to sell goods or services without the page being marked as a Sponsored Link (a paid advertisement). If you, for example, search for electronic consumer goods such as digital cameras, laptops, blu-ray players, you often find that many of the top results are commercial sites.

Commercial pages are often optimized to get a high ranking. This means that they may get a high rank, even if their content is not of high relevance to your search. If the first results page for your search is dominated by commercial pages, you may want to reduce their number.

By selecting **Fewer shopping sites**, you get rid of many commercial sites. They are then given a lower ranking, so that pages with non-commercial information are displayed higher up on the results list. You may find this useful, when you primarily want to find informational pages.

Commercial pages as defined here differ from Sponsored Links. You can read about sponsored links page 83.

Figure 2-52   Displaying more shopping sites

More shopping sites
If you primarily are interested in shopping possibilities, you may want to select **More shopping sites**. The commercial pages will then appear higher on the results list. Maybe more importantly, you'll also see the prices quoted on the results page. You find the prices to the right just below the blue title link (Figure 2-52). The display of the prices is a Rich Snippet feature (see also the box on page 64).

When I tested this feature, Sponsored links on the top of the page apparently also occurred more frequently, but I don't know, if this is a consistent feature.

Page previews
At the introduction of this feature, it was named More text. Later, the name was changed to Page preview. When you select **Page preview**, Google displays a longer snippet. The snippet is the short resume of the content of the page displayed just below the link to the page (page 64). In the standard view, the snippet text is only about 20 words. In the Page previews mode, the snippet is longer (Figure 2-53, page 103). The number of words varies, but often it contains about 80 words. By selecting Page previews, you get much more information directly on the results page. This makes it easier to see if the results page is relevant to your search.

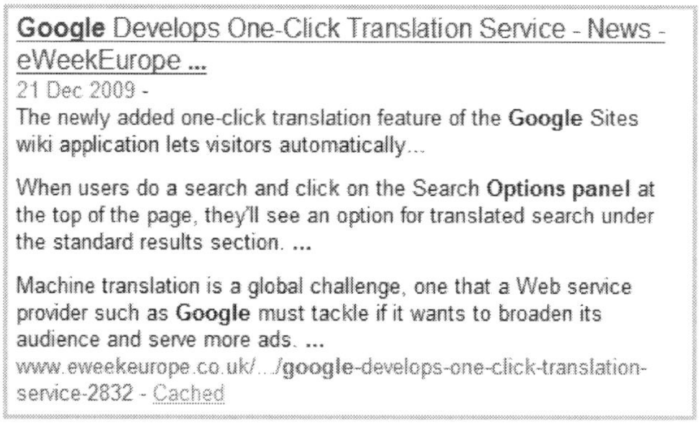
Google Develops One-Click Translation Service - News - eWeekEurope **...**
21 Dec 2009 -
The newly added one-click translation feature of the **Google** Sites wiki application lets visitors automatically...

When users do a search and click on the Search **Options panel** at the top of the page, they'll see an option for translated search under the standard results section. **...**

Machine translation is a global challenge, one that a Web service provider such as **Google** must tackle if it wants to broaden its audience and serve more ads. **...**
www.eweekeurope.co.uk/.../**google**-develops-one-click-translation-service-2832 - Cached

Figure 2-53 A snippet in the Page preview mode

Translated search

The Translated search mode gives you access to Translated search. You can read about Translated search on page 70.

Combination of Modes

As you have seen, the Options panel contains five groups of modes (Figure 2-30, A, B, C, D, and E, page 84), which we here call Results, Time, Location, View, and Display mode. You can combine options from the different modes. Depending on your choices, some options may not be available. As an example, for the search *digital camera* you may select the following combination of options from three different modes (Figure 2-54, page 104):

- Discussions
- Past week
- Page previews

This way, you get discussions, which are not older than one week. The results are displayed with a long snippet (Page previews). You can see the selections you have made in the Statistics bar (Figure 2-54). You can always easily get back to the standard display of the results page by clicking Reset options at the bottom of the Options panel (Figure 2-54).

Summing Up

Google displays the results it finds in response to your query on results pages. As standard, Google displays 10 results per page. You may choose to get 10, 20, 30, 50, or 100 results displayed per page by modifying the Search settings (page 180).

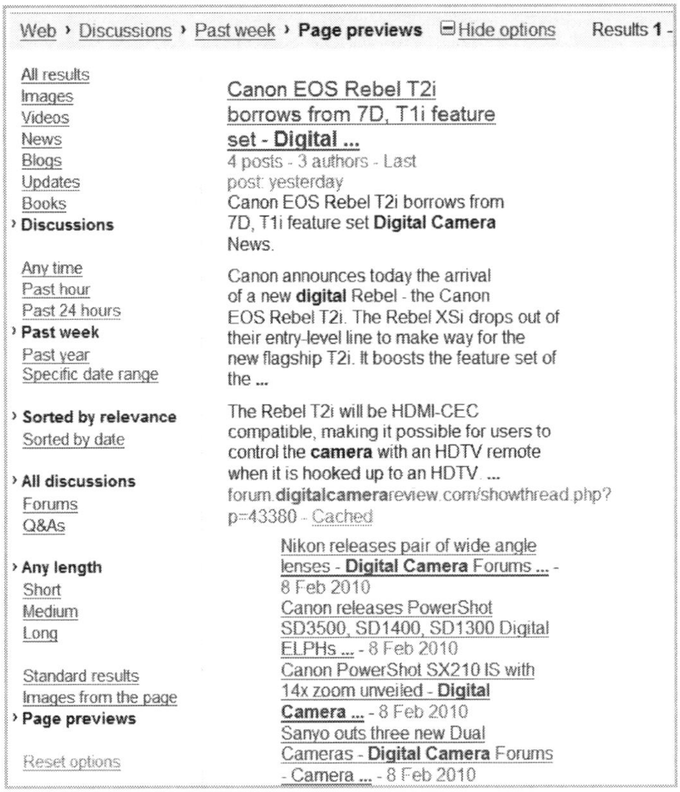

Figure 2-54   Combination of options from different modes

Each search result is a Web page. Each result consists as a minimum of the page title, a snippet, and the page's URL address. You get to the page by clicking the page title.

The snippet gives you a brief description (about 20 words) of the content of the page. You can get a longer description (about 80 words) of the content by selecting Page previews. Google has introduced a new feature called Rich Snippet. In future, we'll most likely get more and more valuable information in the snippet. Today, you can find ratings of goods and services, prices, and so on.

The URL address tells you where the Web page is located. To the right of the URL address, you usually find a link named *Cached*. The link takes you to the cached version of the Web page. It is a snapshot of the page exactly as it looked when the Googlebot last visited the page. Your search terms are highlighted in different colors, making it easy for you to see where each search term is mentioned.

104

At the bottom of the results page, you find a bar, which we here call the Google Page bar or just the Page bar. You use the Page bar to browse between the results pages.

Besides displaying the results from your search, the results page also offers many possibilities for modifying and refining your search. Among other things, the results page contains two identical search boxes - one on the top of the page and one at the bottom. Each search box contains the keywords from your initial search. You can easily modify your search be adding new keywords, deleting one or more of the original keywords, or modify your first query in other ways. Besides adding, deleting, or modifying the keywords, you can also include operators to make your search more focused or to expand it.

The number of Web pages written in other languages than English is rapidly increasing. Often, you may benefit from searching within several languages. In 2009, Google made it much easier to search within several languages at the same time. Today, you can use the tool named Translated search to search within several foreign languages at the same time. Google as standard do all the work of translating your query to other languages, finding results in these languages, and translating the results back into English again. If you want, you can take control over each step and decide, which foreign languages to include, how to translate your query, and so on.

Google Web Search is available in many languages in addition to the US Google Homepage. If you live outside the US and have another language than English as your primary language, you often benefit from searching from your local homepage and using your primary languages as the interface language. This way, you get more local results on the top of results list.

Google as standard looks for relevant results in the entire Web collection of documents. This means that all sort of results are displayed: pages with text information, images, blogs, books, forums, and so on. You can choose to see only one type of results, for example, News, at a time. To restrict the results displayed to a particular type, you just click on the type of results you want on the Navigation bar of the top of the results page. Alternative, you can open the Options panel (see below) and select the type of results you want displayed from there.

In 2009 and early 2010, many significant improvements of Google Web Search were introduced. One of the most important is the Options panel. In the Statistics Bar, you find a Plus button *Show options*. When you click on the button, you get access to many options for filtering, expanding, or otherwise modifying your search. Among other things, you can filter the results by type and time. You can also decrease or increase the number of results from shopping sites. The Options panel, moreover, gives you some possibilities for expanding your search, for example, by using the Related searches, or the Wonder wheel option.

Late in 2009, Google also introduced the possibility to get real-time results displayed as part of the Web search. Earlier, you had to use Google News. You now have two possibilities to get real-time news. If you want to see real-time news from all sources providing real-time information, you just have to select the time filter Latest. If you want to see only the latest updates from Web 2.0 services such as Facebook and Twitter, you can select the option Updates.

In 2009, Google did a lot of experiments with the user interface. Among other things, the Options panel and the real-time search options discussed above were added. While this in the end often benefits you as a user, some users found the many changes somewhat annoying.

The structure and use of the Web are evolving rapidly. You should be prepared that new features may be introduced and well-known features may disappear. In general, the new features will make it easier for you to find what you need.

Chapter 3

Using Advanced Search

The Advanced Search form offers you many possibilities for specifying your query in details. It can assist you in making complex queries. The Advanced Search form makes it easy for you to focus or expand your search, as you want.

Many of the tasks, which you can do on the Advanced Search form, may also be done by use of operators in the simple search box. However, when you use the Advanced Search form for complex queries, you don't have to think about operator names or operator syntax. If you don't like to work with operators, the Advanced Search form is a great tool for making very detailed and specific searches.

In this chapter, we discuss the Advanced Search form. In the next chapter, you'll learn how to use the operators. However, you already here get an introduction to operators, which you can use as an alternative to some of the features on the Advanced Search form. It may make it easier for you to understand, when you may benefit from using an operator instead of the Advanced Search form.

You get to get to the Advanced Search form by clicking the button **Advanced Search** (Figure 3-1). You find the button just to the right of the simple search box.

Figure 3-1   Getting to the Advanced Search form

Anatomy of the Advanced Search Form

We can divide the Advanced Search form into four parts (Figure 3-2), which we here for easy reference call A, B, C, and D. In this section, you get an overview of the Advanced Search form. We go through all the details in later sections in this chapter.

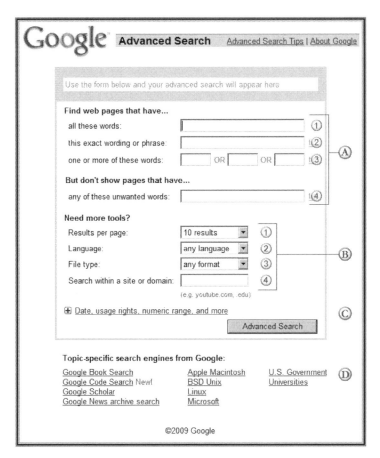

Figure 3-2   Google Advanced Search form

Part A gives you the possibility to specify that all keywords (Figure 3-2, A1), an exact phrase (Figure 3-2, A2), or one or more of the keywords (Figure 3-2, A3) must occur on the results pages. You can also use this section to exclude one or more unwanted keywords from the search (Figure 3-2, A4).

Part B offers you some mixed tools. In the first box (Figure 3-2, B1), you can set the number of results to be displayed per page. In the second box (Figure 3-2, B2, page 108), you can select the search language. In the third box (Figure 3-2, B3), you can restrict your search to a specific file type. In the fourth box (Figure 3-2, B4), you can restrict your search to a specific site or domain.

Part C is at first only a Plus button (Figure 3-2, C). When you click the Plus button, the Advanced Search form expands (Figure 3-3).

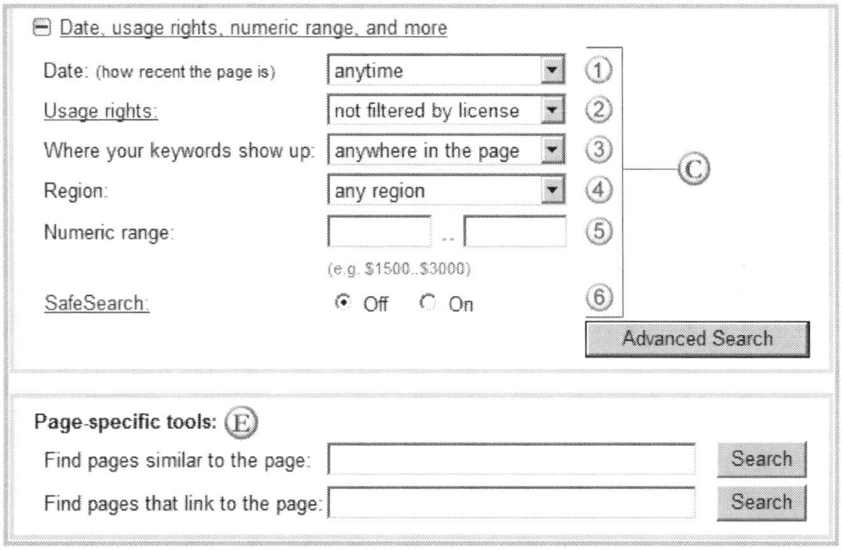

Figure 3-3   Advanced Search form – expanded view

You now get access to six additional filters: Date (Figure 3-3, C1), Usage rights (Figure 3-3, C2), Keyword occurrence (Figure 3-3, C3), Region (Figure 3-3, C4), Numeric range (Figure 3-3, C5), and Safe filtering (Figure 3-3, C6). You can read about each of these filters in later sections in this chapter. Furthermore, a new part, containing two page-specific tools, opens up (Figure 3-3, E).

Part D is found below the proper Advanced Search dialog box (Figure 3-2, D). Google calls this part *Topic-specific search engines from Google*. Among other things, you here get access to Google Book Search, Google Code Search, U.S. Government Web pages, and Universities.

When you have finished filling in the various fields on the Advanced Search form, remember to press the button **Advanced Search.**

Finding Pages with One, More, or All Keywords

When you enter keywords into the simple search box, Google assumes you want to find only the Web pages containing all the keywords. If you want to find an exact phrase, you can do this by enclosing the phrase in quotation marks. This is as far as you can get with the simple search box – unless you want to use operators.

The Advanced Search form gives you more options. You can specify, if you want to find pages with all your keywords (Figure 3-4, A1), with an exact phrase (Figure 3-4, A2), or with one or more of the keywords (Figure 3-4, A3). You can also choose to eliminate a keyword completely from the results (Figure 3-4, A4). More importantly, you can combine these options. This makes the Advanced Search form a powerful tool, with which you can make very complex searches without having to know about operators.

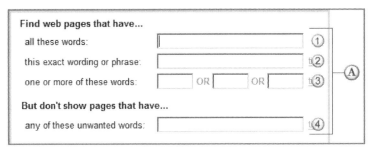

Figure 3-4   Finding pages with one, more, or all keywords

Find Pages with All the Keywords

If you want to find Web pages containing all your keywords, just enter them into the search box *all these words* (Figure 3-4, A1). You get the same results as when you enter the keywords into the simple search box.

Find Pages with an Exact Phrase

In the next search box, *this exact wording or phrase* (Figure 3-4, A2), you can enter a specific phrase, for example, *google search engine*. Google then finds the pages containing exactly this keyword sequence or phrase. You get the same results as when you enter the keyword sequence in quotation marks ("*google search engine"*) in the simple search box.

110

Find Pages with at Least One of the Keywords

In the third line, *one or more of these words*, you find three search boxes (Figure 3-4, A3, page 110). In each box, you can enter a keyword or an exact phrase. Google then finds the pages, which contain at least one of the keywords (or keyword sequences). If you, for example, enter *apple*, *orange*, and *banana* in the three boxes, it finds pages containing at least one of the three words *apple, orange,* or *banana*, but not necessarily all of them.

> **The OR operator**
> As you can see (Figure 3-4, A3), the three boxes are separated by an OR. Google hereby indicates that it uses the OR operator to separate the three keywords or phrases. When you use the simple search box, you can also search for pages containing one result more of the keywords by using the OR operator. The OR operator is a very useful tool. You can read how to use it on page 146 to page 147. When you use the Advanced Search form, you don't need to think about how to use the OR operator.

Don't Show Pages with this Keyword

In the last of the four boxes (Figure 3-4, A4), you can enter words you don't want to occur on the results pages. You can't use this box alone. You must enter one or more keywords in one of the other boxes.

Entering words in the "unwanted words" search box field corresponds to use of minus (-) operator in the search box (page 145).

Advanced Search versus Simple Search

Let us look at the pros and cons of using Google Advanced Search instead of the simple Google search:

- If you just want to find pages that contain all your keywords, there is no advantage in using Google Advanced Search. In contrast, you lose the opportunity to get help from Google Suggest (see page 18).
- If you want to find pages containing at least one of your keywords, but not necessarily all of them, you may find it easier to use the Advanced Search form. You don't have to worry about where to put the OR operator – or to remember to type it with capitals! Please note that Advanced Search form only offers

three search boxes for entering keywords to be separated by OR (Figure 3-4, A3, page 110). If you want to search for more than three alternatives, you must use the simple search box search and the OR operator.

- If you want to exclude a single keyword from your search, it may be easiest just to put a minus before the word. However, if you want to exclude several keywords or key word sequences, it is probably easiest to use the Advanced Search form.

You can easily go from a simple search to an advanced search
If you - after a simple search - find out that you may need to use the Advanced Search form, you don't need to re-type your query. Just click on **Advanced Search**. Google then automatically puts your query into the right boxes on the Advanced Search form.
The keywords are transferred to the search box *all these words* (Figure 3-4, A1).
An exact phrase within quotation marks is transferred to the search box *this exact wording or phrase* (Figure 3-4, A2) – without the quotation marks.
Keywords after an OR operator is transferred to the search box *one or more of these words* (Figure 3-4, A3).
A keyword after a minus sign is transferred to the search box *unwanted words* (Figure 3-4, A4).

Modify Your Search

The second part of the Advanced Search form is *Need more tools?* (Figure 3-5, page 113). You can here choose:

- Number of Results per page to be displayed (Figure 3-5, B1)
- Language of Web pages to be searched (Figure 3-5, B2)
- File type (Figure 3-5, B3)
- Site or domain to be searched (Figure 3-5, B4)

Number of Results per Page

Google as standard displays 10 results per page. You can change this number for all your searches under Search settings (Global preferences, page 180). The settings you make under Preferences apply to all your searches. If you want to change the number of results displayed for your current search only, you can do this on the Advanced Search form (Figure 3-5, B1).

On the Advanced Search form, you can choose between the values 10 (the standard value), 20, 30, 50, and 100 results per page. These are the same values as offered when you set number under Global preferences (page 180).

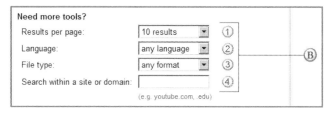

Figure 3-5   Advanced Search form – Need more tools?

The URL parameter Num
If you want other values than 10, 20, 30, 50, or 100, you can change the parameter value Num in the URL string (see page 180). This way, you can choose any value between 1 and 100.

The new value is valid until you reload your browser (see below). As an example, let us assume you have set the value to 20 results per page under Global preferences (page 180). You now change the value to 50 results per page on the Advanced Search form (Figure 3-6). This value applies only to your current search session. When you start a new search session (close and open your browser), the general value 20 becomes valid again.

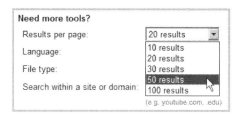

Figure 3-6   Changing the number of results per page from 20 to 50

Note that the *Results per page* box displays the setting you have made under Global preferences. In this example, it is 20.

Languages

When you load the US Google Homepage, Google searches for Web pages written in any language.

Google apparently prefers pages in English (see Figure A-5, page 175). Google has as standard checked the box English under *Prefer pages written in these language(s)*. You can change the preferred search language on the Advanced Search form (Figure 3-5, B2, page 113).

Select your Search language on the Advanced Search Form
Before, it made no difference, whether you set the search language under Global preferences or on the Advanced Search form. However, Google recently has changed the way the two settings work. When you select any other search language than English under Global preferences (Figure A-5, page 175), Google continues to search for Web pages in English - in addition to the language, you select. If your search term is an English word used internationally, Google often finds many more pages in English than in the selected language.

To avoid this, set the search language on the Advanced Search form. This way, the majority of the pages you get are usually written in the language you ask for.

How to Select the Search Language
1. Click **Advanced Settings** (Figure 3-1, page 107).
2. Click the arrow to the right of the Language box (Figure 3-5, B2).
3. Select the search language (Figure 3-7). In Figure 3-7, French is selected as search language. Remember to click the **Advanced Search** button. Google now only searches the Web pages in the selected language.

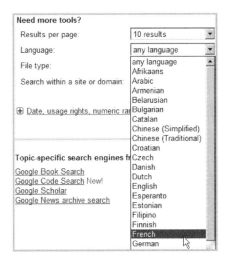

Figure 3-7   Selecting a search language – here French

114

Note that the interface language still is English (Figure 3-8). Google informs you that it now searches French pages – meaning pages written in French (as far as Google "knows").

When you select the search language on the Advanced Search form, Google tries to search and display results from Web pages written in the selected language only.

Remember that the settings you make under Advanced Search form are valid for your current search session only. If you want to use the same search language in your next session, you have to select it anew.

Figure 3-8   Search restricted to French pages

File Type

The possibility to limit the search to specific file types is probably not very much used. However, when you start to use it, you may find this option to be of one of the more valuable features of Advanced Search. The reason is that we often use different file formats (file types) for different tasks. Advanced Search offers you to restrict your search to one of 10 file types (at a time). The 10 file types are (Figure 3-9, page 116):

- Adobe Acrobat PDF (.pdf)
- Adobe PostScript (.ps)
- Autodesk DWF (.dwf)
- Google Earth KML (.kml)
- Google Earth KMZ (.kmz)
- Microsoft Excel (.xls)
- Microsoft PowerPoint (.ppt)
- Microsoft Word (.doc)

115

- Rich Text Format (.rtf)
- Shockwave Flash (.swf)

As you'll learn later, you can search for many more file types - and for more than one file type at a time - by using the simple search box and the operators *filetype* and *OR*.

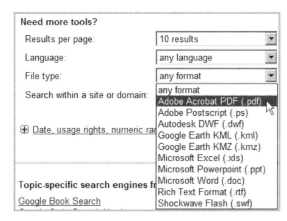

Figure 3-9   Restricting the search to one file type only – here PDF

How to Restrict the Search to a Specific File Type
1. Click **Advanced Settings** (Figure 3-1, page 107).
2. Click the arrow to the right of the File type box (Figure 3-5, B3, page 113).
3. Select the file type (Figure 3-9). In Figure 3-9, the file type Adobe Acrobat PDF is selected. Click the **Advanced Search** button

How to search for file types not listed

Although you can only select ten different file formats from the file type box on the Google Advanced Search form, you can actually ask Google to find dozens of different file formats. Today, there exist more than 2000 different file types (file extensions). It is likely that the Google document database contains at least one Web page of each existing file type. It is not known exactly how many of these file types you can specifically search for, but you can search for all reasonably common file types.

If you want to search for a file type, which is not included in the list of the 10 file types on the Google Advanced Search form, you will have to enter the advanced operator *filetype* followed by the file type extension (see page 159).

116

Why Search for Specific File Types

Different file types are often used for different types of information. As a result, you may benefit from restricting your search to a specific file type.

Below, we are going to take a closer look at four of the 10 file types, you can select. The four file types are .pdf, .xls, .ppt, and .doc. Although there are no definitive rules for which type of information you find in a given file type, you may find the rough guidelines below useful.

Adobe Acrobat PDF (.pdf)

If you restrict your search to the Adobe PDF file type, you will usually find well-prepared and often detailed discussions of the topic you would like to know more about. A PDF file is often the result of a careful thinking and writing process. Restricting your search to PDF files also may be a good way to get access to official documents, white papers, technical reports, manuals, thesis, and a lot of other useful stuff.

You may also find information of high quality in other file formats, such as Microsoft Office .doc.

Be aware, that much of the material you find by restricting your search to PDF file will not be found, if you just make your search without restricting it to the PDF file type. The reason may be that the information found in PDF files often doesn't score high in popularity. Pages with a low general popularity score are displayed at the bottom of the results list – if they are displayed at all.

Note that many PowerPoint presentations are stored as PDF files on the Web. When you restrict your search to PDF files, you may find many PowerPoint presentations. The content of a PowerPoint presentation often differs from the content of a "proper" PDF document (see below).

Microsoft Office Word (.doc or .docx)

Microsoft Office (MS) Word is today the most used word processor program. Until version Word 2003, the documents were stored in a file format called .doc. From Word 2007, Microsoft has introduced a new document file format called .docx (a compressed XML file format). When you select the file type Microsoft Word (.doc) on the Advanced Search form, Google seems to find only the .doc files– and not the new .docx files.

How to search for MS Word .docx files

However, Google does recognize the .docx file type. You can search for .docx files by entering your keywords in the simple search box followed by *filetype:docx*. If you want to find both .doc and .docx files at the same time, type *filetype:docx OR filetype:doc* after your keywords (Figure 3-10). In general, you should only search for one file type at a time to avoid that a rarely used file type "drowns" in the results for a popular file type. There are still about 10 times as many .doc files as .docx files on the Web.

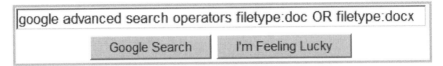

Figure 3-10   Searching for the Word file types .doc and .docx

The information you find in Word .doc and .docx format is frequently as valuable as information found in PDF files. If you want to find as much information as possible about your topic, try searching for PDF, .doc, and .docx files. As mentioned above, it is best to search for one file type at a time. This way, you will get three different results pages with the most relevant and popular documents on the top of each list.

Microsoft Office PowerPoint (.ppt or .pptx)

PowerPoint presentations have become very popular for educational, academic, and business presentations. If you are looking for an introduction to a topic, a PowerPoint presentation may be a good starting point. However, you should note that, in contrast to PDF and Word documents, many PowerPoint presentations are not "standalone" documents. They are often made as a supplement to an oral presentation. This may make some PowerPoint presentations difficult to understand for an "outsider".

How to search for MS PowerPoint .pptx files

From PowerPoint 2007 Microsoft has introduced a new Power-Point file format .pptx. When you select the file type Microsoft PowerPoint (.ppt) on the Advanced Search form, Google seems to find only the .ppt files - and not the new .pptx files. However, Google does recognize the .pptx file type. You can search for .pptx files by entering your keywords in the Google search box followed by *filetype:pptx*.

As noted above, many PowerPoint presentations are stored on the Web as PDF files. If you want to find these documents, restrict your search to the .pdf file type, but include the word *powerpoint* as a keyword.

Microsoft Office Excel (.xls or .xlsx)

Spreadsheets such as Microsoft Excel are primarily used for information, which can be handled and stored as numbers. If you are looking for numerical information such as statistics, economical data, and finance information, you may find it useful to search for .xls files.

> **How to search for MS Excel .xlsx files**
> From Excel 2007 Microsoft has introduced a new Excel file format .xlsx. When you select the file type Microsoft Excel (.xls) on the Advanced Search form, Google seems to find .xls files only – and not the new .xlsx files. However, Google does recognize the .xlsx file type. You can search for .xlsx files by entering your keywords in the Google search box followed by *filetype:xlsx*.

Search within Site or Domain

The last option you may select under *Need more tools?* (Figure 3-5, page 113) is *Search within a site or domain* (Figure 3-5, B4). You may use this box when you want to restrict your search to a domain or a site. Google gives you two examples, namely *youtube.com*, which is a site, and *.edu*, which is a domain.

Restriction of a search to a domain or a site is often a great way to focus your search. If you, for example, want to read about the "official" opinion (in the US) within health issues, you may restrict your search to the domain *.gov*. The *.gov* domain is restricted to US government organizations at the federal, state, and local level.

You can also choose to restrict your search to a specific company, for example, Google, by entering *google.com*. This may be useful, if you want to find out what Google writes about their technologies.

Domain Name Structure

To be able to use this function effectively, you need to have some knowledge about the domain name structure. Most importantly, you should know that some top-level domains are restricted to use by people, who are employed by or have an affiliation to an organization.

Top-Level Domains

A top-level domain name consists of the letters, which follow the last dot in a simple Web address. For example, the top-level domain in www.google.com is .com. The top-level domains can be divided into two main groups: Generic Top-Level Domains, which can be used in all countries, and Country-Code Top-Level Domains, which can be used only by the country in question (for example .de for the domains belonging to Germany).

Sponsored Top-Level Domains

The Generic Top-Level Domains can again be divided into several groups, of which the most important for our discussion is the Sponsored Top-Level Domains. These domains can only be used by people, who are employed by or have an affiliation with the sponsors or organizations, which are served by or controlled by the sponsor. This may sound complicated, but is actually quite simple. For example, the .gov domain can only be used by government agencies within the United States at the federal, state, or local level. The four best-known Sponsored Top-Level Domains are listed below.

Sponsored top-level domains

Domain	Users
.edu	Post-secondary education institutions (colleges, universities), primarily in the U.S.
.gov	U.S. Government entities and agencies, primarily federal.
.int	International organizations, offices, and programs, authorized by two or more nations.
.mil	U.S. military

Each top-level domain has subdomains. For example, you find the subdomains for the Center for Disease Control (CDC), *cdc.gov* under the top-level domain *.gov*.

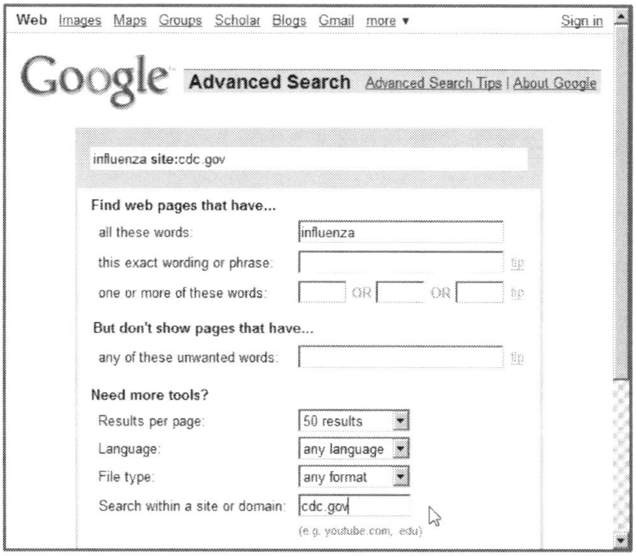

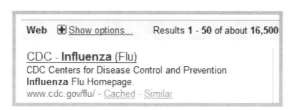

Figure 3-11   Searching within a domain, here the cdc.gov domain

The sponsored top-level domain .gov

If you're looking for high authority sources, for instance, within health, medical conditions, and diseases, you may want to restrict your search to *cdc.gov*. As an example, if you want to get official, reliable information about influenza, you enter *influenza* in the keyword search box and *cdc.gov* in the site search box (Figure 3-11). The very first result is the CDC (Center for Disease Control) influenza page (Figure 3-12).

Figure 3-12   Search result number one is the official CDC influenza page

If you don't know which subdomain to search, you can get an overview by entering your keyword, for example, *health*, in the keyword search box and the domain of interest, here *.gov*, in the site search box. Among the top-ten results, you find some of the most important health information sites in the U.S., including the key portal www.health.gov (Figure 3-13, page 122).

Figure 3-13   Using a keyword to find relevant subdomains

Don't miss the official sites!

Today, when anybody with access to the internet can publish on the Internet, it may be difficult to evaluate the reliability and quality of information you get. In such situation, it may be worth visiting the official sites to get an overview and see, what their point of view is on your topic.

Furthermore, the Web pages with the most reliable information are not necessarily the most popular. They may, therefore, not be displayed on the top of the results list, unless you restrict your search to a domain or a site.

The sponsored top-level domain .edu

The *.edu* top-level domain is as mentioned restricted to use by people employed by or having an affiliation with a post-secondary education institution such as a college or university – primarily in the U.S. Restricting your search to the *.edu* domain is another good way to find reliable information of high quality. In this domain, you can find information about practically any academic and technical topic you can imagine.

You'll primarily find information at the university level. If you want to find stuff at an introductory, but still high level, you may try to add keywords such as *tutorial*, *primer*, or *introduction*. It is important that you enter the additional keywords in the alternative search box (one or more of these words) on the Advanced Search form see example below (Figure 3-14).

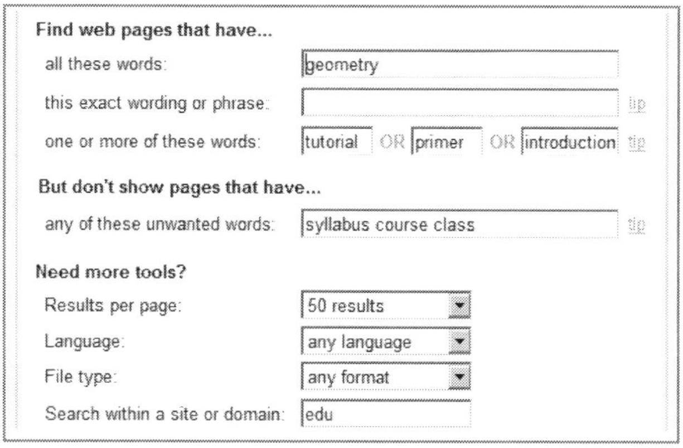

Figure 3-14   Focusing the search by use of qualifying keywords

The risk of using the above qualifying search words (*tutorial* and so on) is that you may get a lot of results describing where and when courses, classes, or lectures are presented. To avoid this, you can try to exclude unwanted keywords such as *syllabus*, *course*, and *class* (Figure 3-14).

If you want to find information at the college level, try specifying this by putting *college* in front of your main keyword. You may, for example, search for *college algebra*. Remember to enter your term, here *college algebra,* into the phrase search box (Figure 3-2, A2, page 108).

Free Top-Level Domains
Besides the restricted top-level domains, there also exist a number of free top-level domains. These domains are not restricted to a specific country. The most important are *.biz*, *.com*, *.info*, *.net*, and *.org*. Domain names within these generic top-level domains are accessible to everybody. In general, there is no benefit in restricting your search to a free top-level domain.

Restriction to Sites
If you want to know something about a particular business, for example, Google, Intel, or Microsoft, you can restrict your search to the sites by entering *google.com*, *intel.com*, or *microsoft.com* into the site search box. If you don't enter other keywords, you'll probably find an overwhelming number of results. Restricting your search to a company site is best done in combination with other keywords, which specify, what your

interest is. To learn about the company in general, entering *investor relations* into the phrase search box is often a good beginning. Under this heading, you typically find information about management, company policies, financial situation, and future plans. Usually, you also get access to the annual reports.

Date, Usage rights, Numeric Range, and More

When you load the Advanced Search form, it contains a condensed menu called Date, usage rights, numeric range, and more (Figure 3-2, C, page 108). Click on the Plus button **Date, usage rights, numeric range, and more** to expand the menu (Figure 3-15).

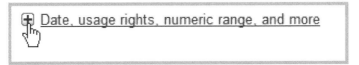

Figure 3-15   Expansion of the menu Date, usage rights, ...

When the menu expands, you get access to six additional filters (Figure 3-3, page 109):

- Date (Figure 3-3, C1,)
- Usage rights (Figure 3-3, C2)
- Keyword occurrence (Figure 3-3, C3)
- Region (Figure 3-3, C4)
- Numeric range (Figure 3-3, C5)
- Safe filtering (Figure 3-3, C6)

Below, we go through each of these filers in details.

Date – How Recent is the Page

On the Advanced Search form, you can only restrict your search to a fixed time period - not a specific date range (see below). You can only choose between four periods – besides *Anytime*. If you want to restrict your search to a specific date range, use the option Filter Results by Time (page 92 to 93).

Searching Results from a Past Period

To restrict your search to a past period, click on the Plus button **Date, usage rights, numeric range, and more** on the Advanced Search form

(Figure 3-15, page 124). Select a period (Figure 3-16) and click the **Advanced search** button (Figure 3-2, page 108).

In the date search box, you can restrict your search to the following five time intervals (Figure 3-16):

- Anytime (no time restriction)
- Past 24 hours
- Past week
- Past month
- Past year

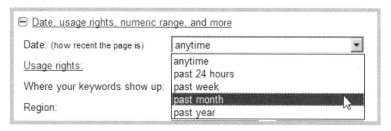

Figure 3-16   Searching results from as past period

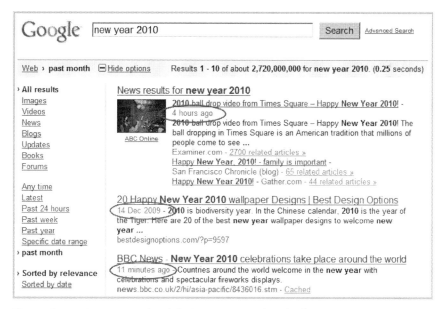

Figure 3-17   Date search with time stamps (circled)

When you restrict your search to a time interval (except *Anytime*), Google places a time stamp in the first line under the heading in each search result (Figure 3-17, circled areas, page 125).

For recent search results, the time stamp gives you the time as minutes ago, hours ago, or days ago, for example 5 minutes ago or 1 hour ago. Google seems to use this type of date stamping for results, which are less than one week old. For older results, Google gives you the date and year, for example, July 1, 2009.

When you select date search on the Advanced Search form, Google opens the Options panel (Figure 3-17). The Options panel gives you access to two additional date search options: Latest and Specific data range. You can read about these options on page 93.

Figure 3-18   Sorting of search results by date

Sorting Search Results by Date
Google presents the results sorted by relevance. You can also get the results sorted by date. Just click **Sorted by date** (Figure 3-18).

Usage Rights
Usage rights are a complex legal topic. It is outside the scope of this book to discuss this topic in details. The short description below is only meant to assist you in understanding the Usage Rights options on the Google Advanced Search. If in doubt, you should seek legal advice – in particular before considering any commercial use of content found on the Internet.

The content – text, music, images, and video – you find on the Internet may be protected by legal rights. There are many different types of legal rights. Before you use, share, or modify any content on the Internet, you should investigate, if the content is protected by any usage rights. The most relevant usage rights are here intellectual property rights, which among other rights include copyrights and trademarks.

126

The Google Advanced Search form offers you some assistance in filtering the search results by Usage rights. Google writes about the Usage Rights filter: *"The usage rights filter on the Advanced Search page shows you pages that are either labeled with a Creative Commons license or labeled as being in the public domain"*. This means that Google relies on the labeling of the material. Below the description of the Usage rights filter, Google gives you the following warning:

> *"Before reusing content that you've found, you should verify that its license is legitimate and check the exact terms of reuse stated in the license. For example, most licenses require that you give credit to the image creator when reusing an image. Google has no way of knowing whether the license is legitimate, so we aren't making any representation that the content is actually or lawfully licensed."*

This means that even though you use the Usage Rights filter, you still have to find out yourself, if you can lawfully reuse the material, you have found on the Internet. In this context, you may benefit from reading the following articles on Wikipedia:

- Copyright (http://en.wikipedia.org/wiki/Copyright)
- Fair use (http://en.wikipedia.org/wiki/Fair_use)
- Public Domain (http://en.wikipedia.org/wiki/Public_domain)
- Creative Commons license (http://en.wikipedia.org/wiki/Creative_Commons_licenses)

Filtering Results by Usage Rights

To restrict your search to a usage rights category, click on the Plus button **Date, usage rights, numeric range, and more** on the Advanced Search form (Figure 3-15, page 124). Select the usage right you want (Figure 3-19, page 128). Click the **Advanced search** button.

The Google Advanced Search gives you the following five options to filter results by Usage rights (Figure 3-19):

- Not filtered by license (no filtering)
- Free to use or share
- Free to use or share, even commercially
- Free to use share or modify
- Free to use, share or modify, even commercially

Google's standard setting is *Not filtered by license*. If you restrict your search to one of the other four options, Google only finds pages with the appropriate license labeling.

Under Advanced Image Search, which is not discussed in this book, Google offers you similar Usage Rights filters.

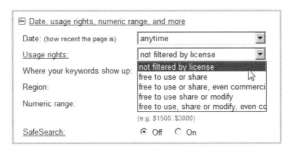

Figure 3-19   Usage Rights filter options

Keyword Occurrence

You can also ask Google to find pages, where your keywords occur in a specific part of the document. Click on the Plus button **Date, usage rights, numeric range, and more** on the Advanced Search form (Figure 3-15, page 124). Select where your keywords must occur (Figure 3-20). Click the **Advanced search** button.

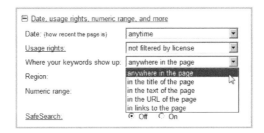

Figure 3-20   Selecting where your keywords must occur

You get the following five options:

- Anywhere in the page
- In the title of the page
- In the text of the page
- In the URL of the page
- In links to the page

128

Please note that you can't combine the keyword occurrence filters with each other on the Advanced Search form. As an example, you can't ask Google to find pages where some of your keywords occur in the title and others in the URL. To do this, you have to use the simple search box and combine your keywords with keyword occurrence operators. You can read about use of the keyword occurrence operators on page 151 to page 158.

The five keyword occurrence filters are described below. The five filters are shown in Figure 3-20, page 128.

Anywhere

The standard setting is *Anywhere in the page*. Google here looks for your keywords anywhere on the document pages in its databases. The standard setting doesn't filter the results by keyword occurrence at all.

In the Title of the Page

Each Web page contains a so-called head section. The head section contains among other things the title element, which - obviously - contains the title of the Web page. The title of a Web page should give you useful information about the content of the document page. This is unfortunately not always the case. As an example, many authors use *homepage, my homepage, page 1*, and similar general names as the page title (Figure 3-21). Despite this flaw, you may find it useful to restrict your search to documents containing your keywords in the title – in particular if you initially get too many hits.

> **The keyword occurrence operator *allintitle***
> When you select the filter *In the title of the page*, Google adds the operator *allintitle* in front of your keywords (Figure 3-21). Use of the operator *intitle* (page 152) gives you more flexibility. By using the *intitle* operator, you can ask Google to look into the title for some of your keywords only.

Figure 3-21   Search for keywords in the title of the page

The text in the Title element is read by the browser, but it isn't shown on the Web page itself. Instead it is shown in the browser's title bar (Figure 3-22).

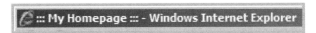

Figure 3-22   The Title element is shown in the browser's title bar

In the Text of the Page

When you ask Google to look for your keywords the text of the page, it actually looks into the so-called body section of the Web page. The body section contains all the text you see on the Web page. It also contains links to the images and other elements displayed on the Web page together with the text. Although it is sometimes stated that use of this search filter excludes pages, where the keywords occur in other places such as the title and the URL, this is not the case. As an example, Figure 3-23 shows a result from a Google for *homepage* using the filter *In the text of the page*. The keyword *homepage* occurs in the snippet, which is here shown in the expanded form (Page preview, see page 102).   The snippet suggests that the keyword occurs in the text as expected, but it also occurs in the title and the URL. When you use the keyword occurrence filters, you don't actually restrict the occurrence of a keyword to a specific location. Rather, you assure that the keyword occurs there, but it may also be found elsewhere.

> ### Superman Homepage - News
> Superman **Homepage** Ringer T-Shirt Superman **Homepage** RingerT-Shirt Now you can show the world that you are a fan of the No. 1 ...
>
> Otherwise just dive right in and jump to the various sections of the Superman **Homepage** by clicking on the navigational links on the left hand side of the screen or those in the "Timeline" menu at the ...
>
> Superman **Homepage** reviewer James Lantz continues reviewing episodes of the 1950s "Adventures of Superman" TV series. ...
> www.superman**homepage**.com/ - Cached - Similar

Figure 3-23   Search for keywords in the text of a page

The keyword occurrence operator *allintext*
When you select the filter *In the text of the page*, Google adds the operator *allintext* in front of your keywords (not shown). Use of the operator *intext* (page 155) gives you more flexibility.

Most often, use of the filter *In the text of the page* will not increase the overall relevance of your search result. However, by using the filter, you avoid getting search results, where one or more of the keywords only occur in the link to the page and not on the page itself (see example in Figure 2-4, page 65, where the word *cached* only occurred in links to the page).

In the URL of the Page

All Web pages have a unique address on the Web, known as the URL address. URL stands for Universal Resource Locator. For our purpose, we can just consider URL to be another name for the page's Web address.

You can ask Google to find pages where one or more of your keywords occur in the URL.

As the keywords in the URL often tell you something important about the page, you may find restriction of your keywords to the URL to be useful. It works somewhat similar to restricting your search to a site (page 119), but there are a few important differences.

Most importantly, when you restrict your search to a domain or site you must enter a valid (existing) domain or site name into the site search box (Figure 3-2, B4, page 108). You may, for example, enter *.com*, or *google.com*. Google then finds all the pages belonging to the domain or site, you have selected.

In contrast, when you restrict your search to a URL by using the *In the URL of the page* filter, Google finds all pages where your keywords occur in the URL. The keywords don't have to occur in a specific sequence or to be part of a valid site name.

If you, for example, enter the keywords, *google, finance*, and *com* into the keyword search box, and select keyword occurrence URL, Google finds all pages where the three keywords occur somewhere in the URL. In this example, Google finds the sites *google.com/finance, google.finance.com,* and a number of Web pages discussing the Google finance sites.

When you use the URL keyword occurrence filter, you usually get a broader variety of search results than when you limit your search to a site.

Figure 3-24   Search for keywords in URL of the page

The keyword occurrence operator *allinurl*
When you ask Google to restrict your search to a URL, it places the operator *allinurl* in front of your keywords (Figure 3-24). As for the *allintitle* operator, there is also a matching *inurl* operator. The *inurl* operator (page 157) gives you more flexibility in writing your query.

In Links to the Page
Probably, the most characteristic thing about Web pages is that you can link from one page to another (external link). You can also link from one place on a page to another place on the same page (internal link), but here we only look at external links.

Web pages are written in the HTML language. When the Web page author inserts a link to an external Web page, a so-called anchor element *<a>* is added to the document. The anchor contains a reference, named *href*, to the external Web page's URL. In the HTML language, Web pages use a code like *<a href="url">link text</a>*. The idea with the link text (also known as anchor text) is to give a description of what you can expect to find, when you click on the link. When you see a link on page, you actually see the link text - not the anchor. It is also the link text you click on.

When you restrict your search to *In links to the page*, you find pages where the keywords occur in link text part of the reference. If you, for example, enter the keywords *Google finance* and restrict your search to pages where *Google finance* occurs in the links, you'll find a number of pages discussing the *google.com/finance* page. Use of the *In links to page* filter may be helpful when you want to find pages discussing a prominent person, a company, a technology, and so on.

If you can't find a keyword in a search result, the reason may be that the keyword only occurs in an external link to the page. An easy way to see, if this is the case, is to view the cached version of the page (see Figure 2-4, page 65).

The keyword occurrence *allinanchor*
When you ask Google to find pages where your keywords occur in the links to the pages, the search engine adds the operator *allinanchor* in front of your keywords. As for the *allintitle* and *allinurl*, there is also a matching *inanchor* operator (page 156), which gives you more flexibility in writing your query.

Be aware that not all link texts accurately reflect the content of the page, which they link to. Also, note that many pages link to themselves. When you restrict your search to pages where the keywords occur in link text, you may get many results, which are of low relevance to your search.

Region

You can also restrict your search to a specific region (Figure 3-3, C4, page 109). Most of the regions are actually countries, but Google uses the term region. You may currently select about 250 different countries and regions.

To restrict your search to region, click on the Plus button **Date, usage rights, numeric range, and more** on the Advanced Search form (Figure 3-15, page 124). Select the region you want (Figure 3-25). Click the **Advanced search** button.

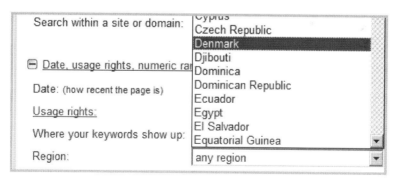

Figure 3-25   Restriction of the search to a region, here Denmark

Restricting your search to a particular country is different from restricting your search to a particular search language. When you restrict your search to a language, you find Web pages written in the language you select. (This is the general idea, but now and then, you get pages written in another language).

When you restrict your search to a particular region, you get pages from the IP address ranges assigned to the region (country).

You may benefit from restricting your search to a region in several ways.

- Different countries may have different views on the same topic and may give different priorities to the same topic. By restricting your search to different countries - one at a time – you often find your topic discussed from different cultural and political points of view.
- You may see Web pages on the first results page, you wouldn't otherwise see. When you restrict your search to a region, Google shows you the most relevant and popular results from the country you select. This means that the top 10 results may be very different from the results you get if you don't restrict your search to a region.
- If you are interested in results from a particular country only, you obviously need to restrict your search to this particular country.

Numeric Range

You can include a numeric range in your search (Figure 3-26). You first enter your keywords, for example, *digital camera*, in the search box or phrase search box. You then enter the start number, the end number, or both in the numeric range search boxes. The numbers may, for instance, be the price range in dollars (Figure 3-26).

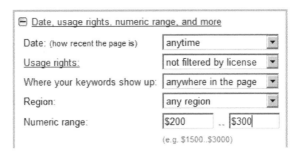

Figure 3-26 Searching for a numeric range

When you enter a number in the first search box only, Google finds pages that contain your keywords and numbers equal to or greater than the number. When you enter a number in the second search box only, Google finds pages that contain your keywords and numbers less than or equal to the number. When you enter a number in both the first and the second search box, Google finds pages that contain your keywords and numbers between the two numbers – including the numbers (Figure 3-26, page 134).

The function seems to work most reliably for the unit $. Avoid entering other currency signs (£, €, and so on) in the numeric range search boxes. Google doesn't always interpret these correctly.

You may enter any type of number: price, years, phone numbers, flight numbers, and so on. You may try to focus your search further by also entering the unit in the numeric search boxes. As an example, you may enter *8am* in the first numeric search box, if you are looking for flights leaving at or after this time. In this example, you would then need to specify the route in the keyword search box on the Advanced Search form, for example *flight boston new york*. Google then adds *8am..* to the query. You may find it easier to use the numeric operator directly in the search box (see page 162).

SafeSearch

Use of the SafeSearch filtering is described under Global preferences (page 179). When you select SafeSearch under Global preferences, it applies to all your searches until you change the setting or override it for a particular search. On the Advanced Search form, you can override your preference setting by selecting SafeSearch Off or On.

Please note that Global preferences give you three options (page 179):

- Use strict filtering
- Use moderate filtering (standard)
- Don't filter my search results

On the Advanced Search form, you can only turn SafeSearch off or on (Figure 3-3, C4, page 109). If you are using Google standard setting, Google applies Use *moderate filtering*.

Page-Specific Tools

When you click the Plus button named *Date, usage rights, numeric range, and more* on the Advanced Search form (Figure 3-2, C, page 108), a new tool box called Page-specific tools becomes visible (Figure 3-3, E, page 109, and Figure 3-27, page 136).

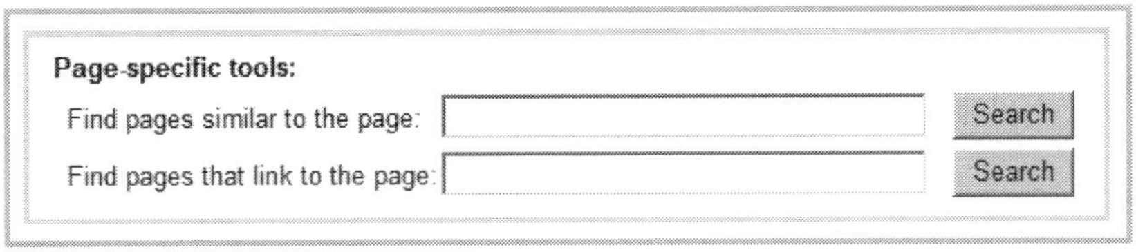

Page-specific tools:		
Find pages similar to the page:		Search
Find pages that link to the page:		Search

Figure 3-27   Page-specific tools

The toolbox contains two tools:

- Find pages similar to the page
- Find pages that link to the page

Find Pages Similar to the Page

To use this tool, enter a valid Web address into the search box *Find pages similar to this page* (Figure 3-28, page 137). You may, for example, enter the US Google page *www.google.com*. Click the **Search button**. Google then tries to find other Web pages with a similar or related content. In this example, Google finds other Web search pages such as www.yahoo.com, www.msn.com, www.wikepia.org, and www. bing.com (Figure 3-28). The use of the Similar pages feature has been summarized very nicely on Google's Australian homepage http://www. google.com.au/help/features.html:

"The Similar Pages feature can be used for many purposes. If you like a particular site's content, but wish it had more to say, Similar Pages can find sites with similar content with which you may be unfamiliar. If you are looking for product information, Similar Pages can find competitive information so you can make direct comparisons. If you are interested in researching a particular field, Similar Pages can help you find a large number of resources very quickly, without having to worry about selecting the right keywords."

This description applies to the link *Similar* that you often find to the right of the URL address of a search result (see Figure 1-19, E4, on page 26). This link works exactly the same way as the tool *Find pages similar to the page*. In both cases, Google adds the operator *related* in front of the Web page's URL address (see circled area in Figure 3-28). You can read about the operator *related* on page 162.

Even though the two tools work the same way, there is a difference in the way, you use them.

136

When you use the *Similar* link on the results page, you first make a search, before you ask Google to find similar pages. In this situation, you need to write a query first, but you don't need to know any Web address.

Figure 3-28   Pages related to www.google.com

When you use the tool *Find pages similar to the page*, you don't make a search first. You just enter a valid Web address in the search box *Find pages similar to the page*. Therefore, you don't need to write a query first, but you must know and enter a valid Web address.

Find Pages that Link to the Page

The *Find pages that link to the page* tool finds pages that link to the page, for which you enter the Web address into the search box. If you, for example, enter *www.google.com*, you find all pages linking to the page www.google.com (Figure 3-29).

Figure 3-29   Pages that link to www.google.com

Note that you only get pages linking to the specific page, for which you enter the Web address. You don't find pages linking to other pages on the same site.

You may enter the Web address without the www or following http://. For example, three addresses www.google.com, http://google.com, and google.com are all valid and give the same results.

The tool works by putting the operator *link* in front of the Web address (see circled area in Figure 3-29, page 137). You can read about the *link* operator on page 161.

Topic-specific Search Engines from Google

At the bottom of the Advanced Search form, you get access to a number of topic-specific search engines (Figure 3-2, D, page 108, and Figure 3-30 below).

Figure 3-30   Topic-specific search engines from Google

Some of these search engines essentially function as filters. If you, for example, select *U.S. Government* and then search for *flu*, you get all pages on the *.gov* domain, on which the word *flu* occurs. You get the same results, if you directly search for *flu site:gov* in the simple search box.

Some of the other topic-specific search engines give you more options than just serving as a filter.

Google Book Search, for example, makes it possible for you to browse through different topics. It also comes with its own Advanced Book Search, which makes it possible for you to make very specific searches for books describing your topic.

Google Scholar is intended for finding academic Web pages and docu-ments. Google Scholar comes with its own preference settings and advanced search features. With these tools at hand, you may write quite detailed searches for academic documents.

It is outside the scope of this book to discuss the specific search engines in details. However, now you know they are there you may want to try out some of the topic-specific search engines.

Summing up

In this chapter, we discussed how you can use the Advanced Search form to make very detailed and specific searches. The Advanced Search form is ideal if you want to make complex searches without having to worry about operators or rules for how to combine them. To find the information you need, you'll seldom need to go beyond the many options the Advanced Search form offers. Below we briefly summarize the things you can do with the Advanced Search form and outline the few weaknesses and limitations it has.

By use of the Advanced Search form, you can search for keywords and exact phrases. You can also use it to find documents, where at least one or more (up to three) alternative keywords occurs, and to omit documents where one or more keywords occur. This part of the Advanced Search form gives you the same search possibilities as you would have if you could use all three Boolean operators AND, OR, and NOT in Google Web Search. Google allows you to search for all combinations of keywords and exact phrases by use of the Advanced Search form - without having to worry about Boolean operators. This is a very significant advantage for most users.

The Advanced Search form also allows you to restrict your search to a specific file type, for example, the PDF file type. However, it only allows you to choose from 10 file types. You can only search for one type at a time. If you want to search for other file types than the ones listed on the Advanced Search form, you have to use the operator *filetype* (see page 159).

Different file types usually contain different types of information. As a result, you may sometimes benefit from restricting your search to one file type.

On the Advanced Search form, you also get the option to restrict your search to a site or a domain. Restriction of your search to one of the sponsored top-level domains, such as .gov, may be useful, if you want to find official documents, read the official points of view, or otherwise find authoritative information. Likewise, it may be useful to restrict the search to a site to find a company's or an institution's official view points.

Even though you can legally read and download a lot of stuff from the Web, you can't be sure that it is legal to reuse the material from the Web. In this chapter, you got a basic introduction to usage rights. You learned that you should be careful to reuse material, in particular for commercial use, before you have checked the relevant usage rights. The Advanced Search form allows you to restrict your search to different types of usage rights – but Google warns you that they don't check the reliability of the usage rights classification of a Web page. You hold the full responsibility for use and reuse of any material you have got from the Web.

The Advanced Search form only offers rather limited possibilities for restricting the search results to a time period. Actually, you may only choose between four pre-defined past periods. A more versatile way to restrict search results to a past period or specific date range is to use the Options panel's time filtering (page 92).

You can also restrict your search to documents where the keywords occur in a specific part of the document (title, text, URL, link to the page). This may be useful in some situations. As an example, we saw that restriction of the search to documents where the keywords occur in the title often eliminates many irrelevant documents.

The Advanced Search form only allows you to restrict the keyword occurrence to the same document location for all query keywords. You can't ask it to look for some keywords in the title and for others in the text. If you need more flexibility, you need to use the keyword occurrence operator. You can read about the keyword operators on page 151 to 158.

You learned that the keyword occurrence operators don't work as a proper filter. In particular, they don't ensure that a keyword occur only in the document part you specify. If you, for example, specify that the keywords must occur in the title, Google finds the documents where the keywords occur in the title – but it doesn't exclude documents where they also occur elsewhere, for example, in the text.

140

Finally, you saw that you can make almost the same settings by use of the Advanced Search form as you can by using Global preferences. The most significant difference is that the settings you make on the Advanced Search form only last as long as your search session. You have to make the settings again, if you close and reopen your browser.

There are a few differences between the settings you can make on the Advanced Search form and under Global preferences. Most importantly, you can't leave out English as search language under Global preferences, unless you also change the interface language (page 175). If you want to exclude English as search language, but at the same time keep it as interface language, you have to use the Advanced Search form (page 114).

Chapter 4

Using Operators

In this chapter, you'll learn how to use operators. An operator is a command you use to tell the Google search engine to do something for you. Google uses two types of operators: the simple operators and the advanced operators. The simple operators are also called the Boolean operators – named after the English mathematician George Boole.

The Boolean Operators AND, OR, and NOT

Before the Google search engine (and other modern search engines) became available, you had to use the Boolean operators AND, OR, and NOT to tell the search engine to find documents with all your keywords (AND) or at least one of the keywords (OR). To exclude documents with keywords, you didn't want, you had to use the operator NOT. You also had to use the correct syntax and sometimes a number of parentheses to ensure that the operators were used in the right order.

With Google Web Search, you can find almost everything you need without having to know about the Boolean operators. When you, for example, want to find pages containing all your keywords, you just enter the keywords in the simple search box (Figure 1-6, page 11). Google then assumes that you want it to find the pages containing all your keywords. You don't have to add the operator AND between the keywords.

If you want to find documents with at least one of the keywords or without one or more specific keywords, you can just use the Advanced Search form, which we discussed in the previous chapter. The Advanced Search form can handle most combinations of Boolean operators without you having to think about operators at all.

It may, therefore, seem as if there is no need to use the Boolean operators any longer. This is also partly correct. Google doesn't "understand" the AND and NOT operators, so don't use these operators at all. You can use the minus operator (-) instead of NOT. In Google Web Search, the minus operator (-) works exactly as the NOT operator in other search engines. You can read about the minus operator (-) below.

There is no substitute for the AND operator in Google Web Search. Google simple assumes that you want to use AND between keywords, when you don't specify anything else. The plus operator (+) can be used to enforce Google to include stopwords, specific spellings, and so on, but is not a substitute for the AND operator. You can read about the plus operator (+) below.

Google understands the OR operator. In Google Web Search, OR works exactly as OR in other search engines. There are many situations, where you may benefit from using the OR operator (see page 48 and page 146 to 147).

The Plus (+) Operator

You may, among other things, use the + operator to:

- include a stopword in your search
- enforce Google to search for a specific word form
- enforce Google to search a word spelled exactly as you type it

Use of the Plus Operator to Include Stopwords

You may force Google to include a word, which Google otherwise might see as a stopword by putting a + in front of the word, for example, *+to*. Don't put a space between + and the keyword. The search string *+to +be +or +not +to +be* "enforces" Google to include *to*, *be*, *or* and *not* in the search. However, as we saw in Figure 1-35, page 52, it is not needed to use the + operator to get Google to find the famous Shakespeare quotation. In general, Google "knows" when to include a stopword, so usually, you don't need to use the + operator for this purpose. You can read about stopwords and the use of the + operator to include stopwords on page 50 to 52.

Use of the Plus Operator to Find Word Forms

Google applies stemming to your search (page 53). If you, for example, search for *bake*, Google also looks for documents containing grammatical variations of *bake* such as *baked* and *baking*. If you only want to find documents containing the keyword itself and not any variations, you may use the + sign to enforce Google to search for a specific word form.

Use of the Plus Operator to Find Words as Spelled

Although the inclusion of differently spelled words is in general useful, it may sometimes give you too many irrelevant results. This particularly applies, if one or more of your keywords contain a non-standard character. Therefore, you may sometimes benefit from enforcing Google to find your keyword exactly as spelled.

Many words, in particular in other languages than English, contain so-called non-standard characters. The standard characters in English are the letters (a to z), the digits (0 to 9), punctuations, and some special characters.

All other characters are non-standard characters. As an example, the letter é is a non-standard character. If you, for instance, want Google to find documents with the word *café* spelled *café* and not *cafe*, you can (as a start, see below) enter *+café*. Even in this simple example, you get very different results with the four different search terms: *cafe, +cafe, café,* and *+café*. You get about 309, 220, 309, and 92 million results, respectively. More importantly, the top 10 results differ significantly. With *cafe* or *+cafe,* the top 10 results included pages about Corporate Average Fuel Economy and Catholic Faith Exploration. With *+café*, these results didn't show up.

Note that some pages include both spellings *cafe* and *café*. To see only the pages with the spelling *café*, you need to "subtract" the pages with the spelling *cafe* by entering: *+café –cafe* (see also the section about the minus operator (-) below).

Use of the + sign to enforce a specific spelling may be important for getting the results you want. If your search for names, you may also benefit from suppression of Google's inclusion of alternative spellings.

The Minus (-) Operator

You may exclude unwanted words from your search by entering the words in the exclude search box (Figure 3-4, A4, page 110). In the simple search box, you can use the minus operator (-) to exclude words from your search. To exclude a word, place a - sign before the word (for example -*wheat*). Don't enter a space between the minus and the word to be excluded. To exclude a phrase, put a minus in front of the phrase. The phrase must be within quotation marks (for example -*"white bread"*).

The minus operator (-) can't be used alone. You must use it together with other keywords or phrases you want to include. If you, for example, enter -*wheat* alone, Google doesn't find any results.

You can exclude as many unwanted words and phrases as you want up to the limit of 32 words in total. The limit includes the keywords and key phrases you do want to find.

You may find the minus operator (-) particularly useful in the following situations:

- to exclude alternative word forms, when Google uses stemming (page 53)
- to exclude a subgroup of results, for example, a subgroup, in which one of your keywords is spelled differently (see the *cafe* versus *café* in the example on page 145),
- to exclude an unwanted word of commercial nature, when you want technical information (see example page 122),
- to exclude unwanted synonyms, when Google automatically includes synonyms (page 48)

The OR Operator

When you enter several keywords in the search box, you narrow down your search. The more keywords you enter the more you restrict your search. While this is in general beneficial, your search may become too narrow, and you may risk overlooking important results. In such situations, you may benefit from expanding your search.

The OR operator may be used as an alternative to Google Web Search's built-in query expansion tools. The built-in tools may do a good job – and often do - but they prevent you from controlling your query. Use of the OR operator may be useful in a number of situations, most importantly:

- to search for different concepts covering essentially the same information need, for example, *weight reduction, weight loss,* or *slimming*
- to include synonyms to one or more keywords in the query in a controlled way, for example, *car, vehicle, auto,* and *automobile*
- to include alternative grammatical word forms in the query, for example, *bake, baked,* and *baking*

- to include alternative spellings of a keyword in a controlled way, for example, *color* and *colour*
- to look for more than one file type in the same query, for example, *.pdf* and *.doc*

Remember to put an OR (in upper-case letters) between each alternative keyword, see also the section Use of the OR Operator in Practice below.

Use of the OR Operator to Include Synonyms

As we have seen (page 48) Google regularly expands your query to include synonyms to your keywords. You may, therefore, wonder if you need to use the OR operator for this purpose. You'll probably find that you often may benefit from using the OR operator for the following reasons:

- Google doesn't always expand your search by adding synonyms to your search query. It may not be easy to find out, if Google has used synonym expansion or not − or which synonyms Google has added.
- Google's rules for when to add synonyms to the query, or for which synonyms to add, are not known. This may lead to unpredictable search results.
- Google may choose other synonyms than you prefer.

By using the OR operator and adding the synonyms you prefer yourself, you can enforce Google to include these synonyms. However, remember that Google still may include other synonyms - both for the keyword, for which you have added synonyms, and for other keywords.

Use of the OR Operator in Practice

When you want to control, which synonyms, word forms, and so on, to include in your search, you can use either the Advanced Search form or the simple box (Figure 1-6, page 11). You can read how to use the Advanced Search form on page 111.

If you want to carry out the search from the simple search box, you must enter the OR operator yourself. Just enter the alternative keywords separated by the OR operator. For three keywords keyword 1, keyword 2, and keyword 3, you would have to enter *keyword1 OR keyword2 OR keyword3*. Google then finds the documents containing at least one of the alternative keywords.

Remember that OR must be written with uppercase letters. There must be a space before and after each OR. You may add as many ORs as you want - up to the 32 keywords limit. The OR operator is not counted as a keyword. This means that you besides a main keyword may have up to 31 alternative keywords separated by OR. In contrast, you can only enter up to three alternative keywords on the Advanced Search form (Figure 3-4, A3, page 110). In praxis, you seldom benefit from searching for more than three synonyms in the same query.

The order of the synonyms doesn't matter. Parentheses are not needed. You can't enforce Google to execute the search in a specific way. Google reads the search string from left to right. On the other side, use of parentheses does no harm, as Google ignores them.

The Advanced Operators

The operators AND, OR, and NOT are often called simple operators. The other operators, which Google uses to carry out many of the functions of the Advanced Search form, are called advanced search operators. In reality, these operators are not more advanced than the Boolean operators are. They just have different functions. When you use the Advanced Search form, you don't have to think about the advanced search operators. Google automatically adds an advanced operator to the query when needed. If you, for example, use the Advanced Search form to restrict your search to the PDF file type, Google adds the advanced operator *filetype* followed by the file extension PDF to you search string as in *filetype:pdf*.

You can carry out most - but not all - of the functions available on the Advanced Search form by use of operators. As an example, there is no operator for restricting the search to a specific region. On the other hand, you can perform some functions with advanced operators, which are not available on the Advanced Search form. As an example, you can search for some keywords in the document title and for other keywords in the document text.

Use of the advanced search operators in the search box gives you the more flexibility than you get on the Advanced Search form. As we saw on page 139 to 141, the Advanced Search form has some limitations.

You can overcome most of its weaknesses by using the advanced search operators in the simple search box.

Benefits of Using Operators

Even though you can do most of the operator-based search tasks from the Advanced Search form without having to worry about operators, you may in some situations benefit from using operators:

- You get access to some advanced search operators, which are not available on the Advanced Search form, for example, *intitle* and *inurl*.
- You can combine operators, which can't be combined by use of the Advanced Search form. As an example, you can combine the *intitle* operator with the *inurl* operator to find documents where some keywords occur in the title and others in the URL.
- When you have got some routine in using the operators, you may find it easier and faster to enter the operators and key-words in the simple search box than to use the Advanced Search form.

If you want to use operators, I recommend that you use them in the simple search box. You may also use them in the search box *all these words* on the Advanced Search form. Don't use them in any other search box on the Advanced Search form. It easily leads to unpredictable or incorrect results.

Using Advanced Operators

An advanced operator is simply an instruction to the Google search engine to do something specific – for example finding documents, where all the keywords occur in the titles of the documents.

We have already looked at some of the advanced operators, when we discussed the use of the Advanced Search form in the preceding chapter. Among other things, you learned that Google places an advanced operator in front of your keywords, when you ask it to find documents where the keywords occur at specific places (title, text, and so on). As you'll see below, you can us the advanced operators yourself in the same way as the Advanced Search form uses them.

Operators Can Do Much, but Not Everything

Be aware that you can't imitate all functions of the Advanced Search form by using advanced operators. The Advanced Search form carries out some of its functions by other means. For these functions, you don't find a corresponding advanced operator. There are, for example, no advanced operators for restricting the search to a specific language or region.

The Four Main Groups of Advanced Operators

In this chapter, we go through all the advanced operators. You'll learn how to best use each operator. The advanced operators may – based on their function - be divided into four main groups:

- Operators for keyword occurrence
  - *intitle*
  - *allintitle*
  - *intext*
  - *allintext*
  - *inurl*
  - *allinurl*
  - *inanchor*
  - *allinanchor*
- Operators for finding filetypes
  - *filetype*
  - *ext*
- Page-specific operators
  - *cache*
  - *info*
  - *related*
  - *link*
- Others

With one exception (the *ext* operator), we only discuss operators that are officially supported by Google. As an example, this means that we are not going to discuss the outdated *daterange* operator.

How to Use Advanced Operators

With few exceptions, all advanced operators are followed by a colon (:). The colon may be seen as a part of the operator, but I have decided not to include it in the operator name. However, remember always to place a colon immediately after the operator name (with the exception of the *weather* operator, see page 167) - with no space between the operator name and the colon as in *intitle:*

In general, there is no space after the colon and the following keyword. The only possible exceptions are the four operators beginning with *all*, for example, *allintitle:*. We here call these four advanced operators the *all** operators. They have in common that they can be followed by more than one keyword. An *all** operator applies to all keywords that follow it. You may put a space after the colon following the operator. However, the space is not needed. It is, therefore, a good search practice always to place the first keyword for these operators immediately after the colon. This way, there is less risk that you happen to put a space after the colon where no space is allowed. Putting a space after the colon abolishes the function of the other advanced operators.

Operators for Keyword Occurrence

You can search for occurrence of your keywords in four different parts of a document (see also page 128):

- Title
- Text
- URL
- In anchor text in links to the document

For each of the four occurrences, there exist two operators of the type *in** and *allin**, where * stands for the location of the keyword(s). This gives eight operators in total:

- *Intitle*
- *Allintitle*
- *Intext*
- *Allintext*
- *Inurl*
- *Allinurl*
- *Inanchor*
- *Allinanchor*

In the next two sections, the general use of the two types of operators, *in** and *allin**, are described. In the sections following this general introduction, you get some concrete examples on use of each type of operator.

151

The In* Type Operator

An *in** operator only applies to the keyword or phrase immediately following it. You must type this operator in front of each keyword that you want to occur in a specific location of the documents. An *in** operator can be followed by a single keyword or a single phrase (in quotation marks).

Remember that the operator must be followed by a colon (:). No space is allowed before or after the colon. The general syntax is *in*:keyword*. You can use several *in** operators of the same type in a query (Figure 4-1). You may also use different *in** operators in the same query, and you can combine the *in* operators* with most other operators. Use of *in** operators gives you much more flexibility in writing your queries than use of the *allin** operators.

The Allin* Type Operator

An *allin** operator applies to all keywords and phrases (in quotation marks) following it.

An *allin** operator must be followed by a colon. No space is allowed before the colon. In contrast to what applies to other advanced operators, a space is allowed after the colon – before the first keyword. You may even have more spaces. The space is not needed. As stated above, you may benefit from not putting a space after the colon following an *allin** operator. This way, the syntax for all advanced operators becomes the same. The simple rule is then: no space before or after the colon. In the screenshot shown in Figure 4-2, page 153, I have on purpose omitted the space after the colon.

Figure 4-1   Use of the intitle operator

The general syntax for a query with three keywords, here called *keyword1*, *keyword2*, and *keyword3*, is *allin*:keyword1 keyword2 keyword3*.

You may use an *allin** operator before a single keyword or before a phrase, but it will then behave exactly as the corresponding *in** operator. You can only use one *allin** operator in a query. You can't mix an *allin** operator with other keyword occurrence operators.

The Intitle and Allintitle Operators

To illustrate the use of an *in** operator and the corresponding *allin** operator, let us look at an example, in which we want to find the documents where the words *bake* and *cake* both occur in the Web page title.

We can do this in two ways. First, we can use the operator *intitle* in front of each of the words *bake* and *cake* as in *intitle:bake intitle:cake* (Figure 4-1, page 152). Alternatively, we can use the operator *allintitle* as in *allintitle:bake cake* (Figure 4-2).

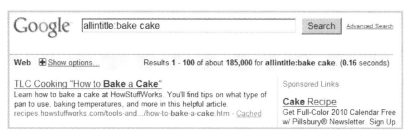

Figure 4-2   Use of the allintitle operator

We get exactly the same results and the same ranking (order) of results in the two cases. However, as mentioned above, the *intitle* operator gives you more flexibility than the *allintitle* operator does.

First, you can choose to search for only some keywords in the titles of the documents. For the remaining keywords, you may either specify another location, for example in the URL (by use of the *inurl* operator, see below), or you can simply omit to specify, where they must occur.

Second, the *allintitle* can't be combined with others of the keyword occurrence operators listed above. For example, you will not find any results, when you enter *allintitle:bake cake intext:banana*. Google will tell you that your search did not match any documents (Figure 4-3, page 154). Actually, there exist more than 10,000 documents, in which *bake* and *cake* occur in the document title and *banana* in the text. However, to find these documents you must use the correct syntax, which here is *intitle:bake intitle:cake intext:banana* (Figure 4-4, page 154).

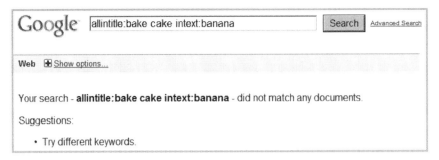

Figure 4-3   Invalid mixing of the allintitle operator with another operator

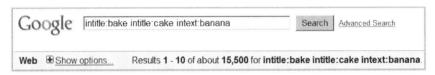

Figure 4-4   Correct mixing of intitle and intext operators

Limiting the search for one or more keywords to the titles of documents often is an effective way to find relevant documents. If a Web page is well structured, its title should clearly state, what the page is about. Although this may not always be the case (page 129), you frequently benefit from restricting your search to the titles of the documents. You may miss some valuable pages, but usually you find the information you need.

Other Keyword Occurrence Operators

In the next three sections, we go through the remaining three pairs of keyword occurrence operators:

- *intext* and *allintext*
- *inanchor* and *allinanchor*
- *inurl* and *allinurl*

As the *site* operator is related to the *inurl* and *allinurl* operators, we discuss the *site* operator together with the *inurl* and *allinurl* operators.

You use the *intext*, *inanchor,* and *inurl* operators the same way as you use the *intitle* operator. The only difference is that Google looks for your keywords in different parts of the documents.

154

You use the *allintext, allinanchor,* and *allinurl* operators the same way as you use the *allintitle*. Again, the difference is that Google looks for your keywords in different parts of the documents. Remember that the *allin** operators can't be combined with other keyword occurrence operators.

The Intext and Allintext Operators

The *intext* operator instructs Google to find documents where the keyword preceded by the *intext* operator must occur in the text, also known as the body text. Each keyword must be preceded by an intext operator. If you, for example, want to search for *bake* and *cake* in the text, you must enter *intext:bake intext:cake.*

If you use the *intext* operator alone, you usually get the same results as when you leave out the operator. The only difference is that use of the *intext* operator ensures that the keyword actually occurs in the body text of the document and, for example, not only in links to the page. In some situations, this difference may be important (see also page 131). You'll have to try out, if it makes a difference for your search.

You may now and then find it useful to combine the *intext* operator with the *intitle* operator. This way, you can ask Google to find documents, in which some keywords occur in the title and others in the text. This may be useful, if searching for documents where all keywords occur in the title gives too few results. In such situations, try to search for the more important keywords in the title of the documents and for the less important in the text (for example, *intitle:bake intitle:cake intext:banana intext:chocolate).*

Note in Figure 4-5 that the keywords *banana* and *chocolate* occur in both the title and the URL, even though we used the operator *intext.* As expected, they occur in the text, but you can't really conclude that from the figure. You need to open the Web page to confirm that they occur in the text – even though they appear in the snippet.

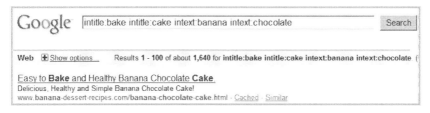

Figure 4-5   Combination of the intitle and intext operators

The important point is that use of the *intext* operator ensures that the keyword occurs in the text. However, it doesn't prevent it from occurring in other places as well. This fact is often overlooked.

The Inanchor and Allinanchor Operators

Most, if not all Web pages contain links to other pages. A link consists of an URL address (which you can't see), and the link text, which is visible and clickable. When you click on a link, you actually click on the link text. This take you to the URL address.

> **The link text is the anchor text – and the other way round!**
> The link text is also known as the anchor text. Today, the term link text is much more common than anchor text. Search engine people, however, often use the term anchor text. The operators are stilled called *inanchor* and *allinanchor*. It may be a little confusing, but just remember that the link text and the anchor text are exactly the same!

A link on a Web page has this general structure (see also page 132):

<a href="url">**Link text**</a>

It could as well be written as:

<a href="url">**Anchor text**</a>

However, the latter form is only seldom used - see the box above.

As an example, the link to Google's US homepage from a regional homepage (for example, the Danish Google homepage) may look like this:

<a href="http://www.google.com/ncr">**Go to Google.com**</a>

When you click on **Go to Google.com** (Figure 4-6), you are taken to the Web page www.google.com/ncr, to which the URL address points.

Advertising Programs - Business Solutions - About Google - Go to Google.com

©2010 - Privacy

Figure 4-6 You can click on a link text, here Go to Google.com

> Don't bother about the *ncr*. It is just a code telling the Google server not to re-direct you to your local homepage again. When you get to the Google US homepage, you only see the Web address http://www.google.com – not the *ncr* part.

Despite the importance of the links for the ranking of a Web page, the operators *inanchor* and *allinanchor* are only seldom useful (see below). Google already gives a high rank to Web pages, for which the inbound links contain the keywords in their link texts. You usually don't gain much by specifying that the keywords must occur in the link text. However, you may find the *inanchor* and *allinanchor* operators useful in a few situations.

As an example, you can try to use the *inanchor* or *allinanchor* operator for reducing the total number of results. It may or may not increase the relevance of the results. You'll have to judge this yourself from case to case.

Figure 4-7   Combining the inanchor operator with -inurl

As another example, you may use the *inanchor* or *allinanchor* operator to find pages discussing companies, stocks, technologies, new discoveries, popular people, and so on. In such situations, you may benefit from excluding pages from the company being discussed or reviewed. As an example, you may use the query *inanchor:"google nexus" –inurl:google* (see next section) to find out what others think about Google's mobile phone (Figure 4-7).

The Inurl, Allinurl, and Site Operators
In general, a Web page owner will try to use a URL address for his or her page, which tells you what the page is about. You may, therefore, use the *inurl* and *allinurl* operators to find pages dealing with a specific topic

such as *google operators* (Figure 4-8). The *inurl* and *allinurl* operators find pages where the keyword (*inurl*) or keywords (*allinurl*) occur somewhere in the URL address. If you, for example, enter *allinurl:google operators*, you get all Web pages where *google* and *operator* occur somewhere in the URL.

Figure 4-8   Example on use of the allinurl operator

The Site Operator
If you want to find the Web pages owned by a person or company, you should use the *site* operator – not the *inurl* or *allinurl* operator. This requires, however, that you know the site name. To find, for example, all Web pages on Google's site google.com, enter *site:google.com*.

When you use the *site* operator, it also lists Web pages in subdirectories. If you, for example, enter *google.com*, it also lists Web pages from www.google.com/finance, www.google.com/analytics, and so on.

The site operator is generally most useful, if you use it in combination with keywords that specify which type of information on the site you are particularly interested in. You may, for example, search for discussion of *advanced operators* on *google.com* sites by entering the query *"advanced operators" site:google.com*.

Differences between the Inurl and the Site Operators
The *inurl* and *site* operators appear to be rather similar. There are, however, some differences. The most important are:

- To use the *site* operator, you must know and enter a valid site name such as *google.com.* To get the *inurl* operator to work, you just need to enter a correctly spelled keyword.
- The *site* operator searches within sites. It includes subdirectories. The *inurl* and *allinurl* operators search for the keywords anywhere in the URL address.

158

- The Web pages found by the *site* operator are in general owned and controlled by one company or one person. The pages found by the *inurl* operator often belong to a broader group of people and companies. By searching for your keyword(s) in the URL, you usually get a more diverse view on your topic than by searching a company site.

The Filetype Operator

As you saw on page 115, you can use the Advanced Search form to search for specific file types. However, you can only search for one file type at a time and only for 10 file types. You get more flexibility, when you use operator *filetype*. This way, you can search for any major file type and for several different file types at a time (by separating each file type with an OR operator). If you, for example, want to find more information about advanced operators in Google, but you only want to get PDF and Word documents, you may enter *"advanced operators" google filetype:pdf OR filetype:doc* (Figure 4-9).

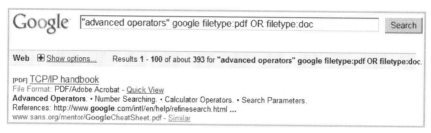

Figure 4-9 Use of the file type operator in combination with OR

Although you may search for as many file types as you want at the same time (up to the limit of 32 keywords), you will in general not benefit from searching for more than two or three related file types such as .pdf, .doc, and .docx, at a time. The *filetype* operator is in general most valuable, when used for a single file type or for two closely related file types. The advantages of searching for some of the major file types are discussed on page 115 to 119.

The *filetype* operator is a powerful restricting operator, as it excludes all other file types.

The Ext Operator

Although not officially supported by Google, you can use the operator *ext* instead of *filetype*. It is a little shorter to type. In my experience, you get the same results as with *filetype*. However, in general, it is best to use the "official" operators. Google may stop supporting "unofficial" operators without notice.

Page Specific Operators

Google offers you four operators, which can give you some information about a Web page. The four operators are:

- *Cache*
- *Info*
- *Related*
- *Link*

The Cache Operator

Google builds it database of information on the Internet by having special software – the so-called Googlebot - searching all Web pages (see also page 31). First time a Googlebot visits a Web page, it copies the information on the page to the Google database. The copy of the information is called the cache or the cached page. The Googlebot regularly visits the page again. If the Web page is updated, the Googlebot updates the cache of the page. The cache is the Web page exactly as it looked, when the Googlebot last visited the page.

For most Web pages, Google offers you the possibility to see both the cached page and the current (actual) version. You get to the cached page by clicking on *cached* in the snippet (Figure 2-3 D, page 64).

When you click on *cached* Google informs you that you are looking at a cached version of the page (Figure 2-4, page 65). It also informs you when the snapshot (the cache) of the page was taken – and warns you that the page may have changed after the snapshot was taken.

The cached page doesn't necessarily contain the most recent information, but may be useful in a number of situations (see page 65 to 66).

You use the cache operator by typing *cache* in front of the URL address. Remember the colon (:) between cache and the URL address. If you, for example, want to see the cached page of the Google US homepage, enter *cache:google.com*. You'll probably seldom use the cache operator this way, because you have to remember the URL address. Typically, you get to a cached page from a search result (see page 65).

160

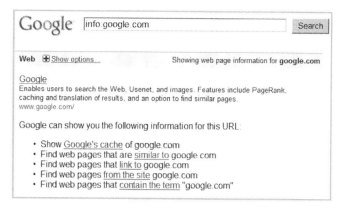

Figure 4-10   The info operator used for google.com

The Info Operator

The *info* operator gives you information about a Web page. The syntax is *info:url*, where *URL* is the Web address. When you, for example, enter *info:google.com* (Figure 4-10), you get information about the main Google homepage. First, you get a very short description of the Web page. Often, this will probably not tell you more than you already know about the Web page. You then get links to various types of the information about the Web page:

- The cached version of the page (see the *cache* operator above)
- Similar pages (see the *related* operator below)
- Pages that link to the page in question (inbound links, see the *link* operator below)
- Web pages from the site, to which the web page belongs (see the *site* operator page 158)
- Pages that contain the term corresponding to the url address (see the example for *info:google.com* in Figure 4-10)

The *info* operator doesn't give you access to any new information or features. You may use it as a convenient shortcut to information you could find with other operators.

The Link Operator

The link: operator finds all Web pages that link to the page. The syntax is *link:url* (Figure 4-11, page 162). The URL must be a valid Web address. When you use the link operator in the search box as in Figure 4-11, you get the same search results as when you enter the Web address into the search box Find pages that link to the page (see page 137). You can read on page 137 what you may use the link operator for.

Note that you only find the pages linking directly to the specific URL address you enter. As an example, if you enter *link:google.com*, you find only the pages linking to www.google.com – not to other Google URL addresses such as www.google.de (Figure 4-11 below).

Figure 4-11   The link operator used for google.com

The Related Operator

The *related* operator is intended to assist you in finding Web pages, which are similar to the one, you already have found. The syntax is *related:url* (Figure 4-12). URL must be a valid Web address.

When you use the related operator in the search box as in Figure 4-12, you get the same search results as when you enter the Web address into the search box Find pages similar to the page (page 136). You can read on page 136 what you may use the *related* operator for.

Figure 4-12   Use of the related operator for google.com

Numeric Range Operators

As you learned in Chapter 3, you can include a numeric range in your search by entering the number or numbers into the numeric range search boxes on the Advanced Search form (page 134). You can also enter the numeric range into the simple search box. You just have to enter the numbers separated by two dots.

The syntax is *nlo..nhi* where *nlo* is the low number and *nhi* is the high number. If you, for example, want to find information about DVD recorders with hard drive capacity between 160 and 320 GB, you may enter the query *dvd recorder gb 160..320* (Figure 4-13).

Figure 4-13   Entering of a numeric range by use of two dots

You can use the two dots to enter a range (*nlo..nhi*), a lower limit (*nlo..*), or an upper limit (*..nhi*).

When you only enter a low number, Google finds the pages with numbers that are equal to or higher than the number. If you, for instance, enter *160..*, Google finds pages with numbers from 160 and upwards. Note that the low number must precede the two dots with no space in between.

When you only enter a high number, Google finds the pages with numbers that are equal to or less than the number. If you, for instance, enter *..360*, Google finds pages with numbers from 320 and downwards. Note that the high number must follow the two dots with no space in between.

In principle, you should get the same search results by entering the two dots into the search box as you get when you enter the number(s) into the numeric range search box on the Advanced Search form (page 134). However, sometimes you may see minor differences.

Be aware that Google sometimes finds pages with numbers in the range you have specified, which are not otherwise related to your search. When you search for *hard drive 500.. gb*, you may, for example, find serial numbers and phone numbers above 500.

Other Advanced Operators

We have now discussed all the proper advanced operators you can use to search for all types of information on the Web.

Besides these operators, Google offers a few more, which differ from the proper advanced operators in various ways (see next section). They may be categorized in four groups:

1. Operators for specific information needs
   o Define
   o Stocks
   o Time
   o Weather
2. Operators used in Google Group search
   o Author
   o Group
   o Insubject
3. Operators used in Google News search
   o Author
   o Location
   o Source
4. Operators usable only in the US
   o Phonebook
   o Rp (Reverse phonebook)

In this book, we focus on Google Web Search. We are, therefore, not going to discuss group 2, 3, and 4 here. Group 1 is discussed below.

Operators for General Information Needs

The four operators *define*, *stocks*, *time*, and *weather* are meant to be used alone. In contrast to the proper advanced operators, they are not intended for restricting or expanding a search based on a query with other keywords. You just use them, as they are, to get some information. Don't try to combine them with other operators.

Define

As the name states, the define operator is intended for getting a definition of word or concept. If you, for example, want to get a definition for the word *spider*, you enter *define:spider* into the search box (Figure 4-14, page 165).

Note that the operator *define* is followed by a colon. There doesn't need to be a space between the colon and the word to be defined, here *spider*, but a space will not do any harm. The operator *define* reads all words after the colon as an exact phrase.

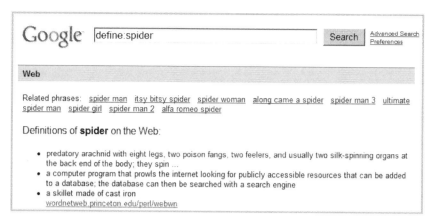

Figure 4-14   Use of the operator define for a single word

Google will, for example, try to find definitions for the phrase "green-house gas", when you enter *define: greenhouse gas* (Figure 4-15). Note that you get many suggestions for related phrases (Figure 4-14 and Figure 4-15). The related phrases often lead you to information that can help you to get your topic described in more details.

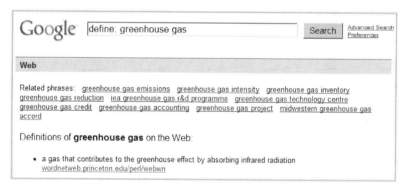

Figure 4-15   Use of the operator define for an exact phrase

Stocks

The operator *stocks* is intended for giving you direct access to information about a stock. If you want to use it, you should - at least in principle - know the correct stock ticker symbol (abbreviation) such as *msft* for Microsoft Inc. However, Google Suggest often helps you to find the ticker symbol. If you, for example, start typing *stocks:mi,* Google guesses that you want to get information about the Microsoft Inc. (Figure 4-16, page 166).

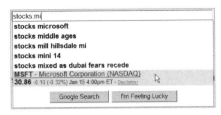

Figure 4-16   Google Suggest finds the right stock information for you

If you don't know the stock ticker symbol and Google doesn't provide sufficient help, you may try the Google Finance homepage instead. On this page, you can enter the company name into the search box. You don't need to know the stock ticker symbol. You get to the Google Finance homepage by entering *http://www.google.com/finance* into your browser's address bar (Figure 1-1, page 5).

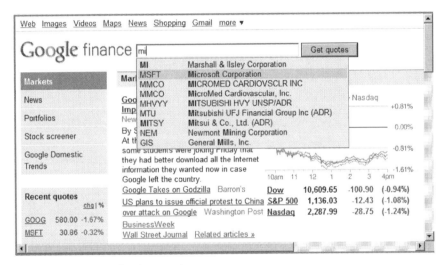

Figure 4-17   Google Finance homepage

Google Suggests also works on Google Finance homepage. As soon as you have typed *mi* into the Google finance search box (Figure 4-17), Google suggests Microsoft Corporation.

Time
The *time* operator gives you the local time for the location you enter. The syntax is *time:location* where *location* is the city or country, for which you want to get the local time. If you enter a country with several time zones, you get a list of the time at the more important locations (Figure 4-18, page 167).

Figure 4-18   Use of the operator time for a country location

Weather

The *weather* operator works similar to the *time* operator. There is, however, an important difference. There is no colon after the operator *weather*. The general syntax is *weather location* – with a space between weather and location (Figure 4-19).

Figure 4-19   Use of the weather operator. Note the absence of a colon!

The operator weather works for most city names. In the US, you may also use a ZIP code. If you want to the weather forecast for Mountain View in California, you can just enter the ZIP code 94043 (Figure 4-20).

Figure 4-20   Use of the weather operator for a US ZIP code

Summing up

In this chapter, we have seen how the simple and advanced operators work, and how you may benefit from using them in various situations. By use of operators, you can do almost the same as you can on the Advanced Search form. In a few situations, use of operators gives you more flexibility than the Advanced Search form offers.

First, we saw that except for the OR operator, the Boolean operators don't play any significant role in Google Web Search. The OR operator is a highly useful tool, which you can use to search for synonyms, different word forms, different spellings, and so on. The OR operator is the best tool you can use for expanding your search in a controlled way.

In contrast, there is no need for using the AND operator at all. Google Web Search assumes that there is an AND operator between two successive keywords - unless you tell it otherwise by use of an operator.

Google Web Search doesn't understand the Boolean NOT operator, but the minus (-) operator has exactly the same function as the NOT operator has in many other search engines. The minus operator (-) may be useful when you want to exclude a specific keyword, alternative word forms, alternative spelling, and so on. The minus (-) operator may also be used for "subtracting" or excluding a subgroup of search results. The minus operator (-) can never be used alone, but it may be highly valuable for focusing a search based on other keywords.

The counterpart to the minus operator (-) is the plus operator (+). The plus operator (+) may be useful for enforcing Google to search for specific words, words forms, spellings, and so on. It may also be used to enforce Google to include a word that otherwise might be treated as a stopword.

You can use the plus operator (+) and minus operator (-) in combination to make highly focused searches for specific words, word forms, spellings, and expressions. It is very easy to use these operators directly from the search box.

Second, we worked through all the advanced search operators. You learned that there is nothing really advanced about them. They are just instructions to Google Web Search to carry out a search in a particular way.

While most of the advanced search operators just mirror functions that are also available on the Advanced Search form, some of them are unique. In particular, the Advanced Search form doesn't have the four keyword occurrence operators: *intitle*, *intext*, *inurl*, and *inanchor*. By use of these operators, you can search for the keywords in the location of the documents you want. You can freely combine the four operators, so you, for example, can search for some keywords in the title, some on the text, and some in the URL. This is often an effective way to focus your search.

The *filetype* operator also gives you more flexibility than the file type search box on the Advanced Search form. As you saw in Chapter 3 (page 116), you can only search for 10 file types on the Advanced Search form - and only for one file type at a time. By use of the advanced operator *filetype*, you can search for hundreds of different file types (extensions), and you can search for more file types at a time. You learned that the *filetype* operator is usually best used to search for one file type at a time, or for two or three closely related file types, for example .pdf, .doc, and .docx.

The *ext* operator has the same function as the filetype operator. Although not officially supported by Google, you get the same results with the *ext* operator as with the filetype operator. You may prefer to use the *ext* operator, as it is shorter to type.

Last, we saw that Google uses a few other advanced search operators in some of its other search programs (Google Group Search and Google News Search). Google also comes with a few operators, you can use to find definitions (of words and phrases), and general information (stocks, weather, and time).

As you have seen in the previous chapters, you can make almost any kind of searches and find most of the information you need by use of the Advanced Search form. However, by using simple and advanced operators directly in the search box, you can often further refine your search in situations where it is otherwise difficult to find the information you need. Furthermore, as you get more experienced you may prefer to use the operators instead of the Advanced Search form (where possible).

Appendix A

Search Settings

The way the Google search page displays information is named Search settings. Google also uses the names Google preferences and Global preferences for Search settings. The Search settings are:

- Interface Language
- Search Language
- Safe Surf Filtering
- Number of Results
- Results Window
- Query Suggestion

Google allows you to modify the Search settings. On the next pages, you learn how to modify each of the settings. As the name Global preferences indicates, the settings you make here (on the Global preferences form) apply for all searches you do. The settings are valid until you change the Global preferences - or until you temporarily change them on the Advanced Search form. Remember that Search settings you make on the Advanced Search form only apply to your current search session. This means that the settings are valid until you end your search session by closing the browser. Once you reload your browser, Google set all settings back to the Global preferences.

Loading the US Google homepage

Before we start, we need to look at the same Google search page in the same language. If you live in US and have the US Google homepage (www.google.com) in English as your homepage, you are ready to go.

If you live outside the US, you should start by loading the Google US homepage and setting the language to English. You can read how to do this on page 5. As you may remember, the easiest and most reliable way to do this is by clicking the link *Google.com in English* (Figure 1-2 B, page 6) on your local homepage. When you click this link, you are taken to the US Google homepage. At the same time, the interface language is usually changed to English.

You can read about interface languages on page 174. Figure A-1 shows the US Google homepage.

Figure A-1   The US Google homepage

Getting to the Search Settings

You get to the Search settings by clicking the link *Search settings* on the top of the US Google homepage (Figure A-1, circled area). You land on the Google preferences page, also known as the Global preferences page (Figure A-2, page 173).

On the Global preferences page, you can as stated above change the following six settings:

- A. Interface Language
- B. Search Language
- C. Safe Search Filtering
- D. Number of Results
- E. Results Windows
- F. Query Suggestions

The letters A to F refer to the labels in Figure A-2. Figure A-2 is only intended as an overview. We go through each setting below, illustrated by more detailed figures, where needed.

The Interface Language

The language the Google search page uses for menu names, text in buttons, etc. is called the interface language. The Google search page is currently available in 129 languages. Of these, 124 are "real" languages (see page 77).

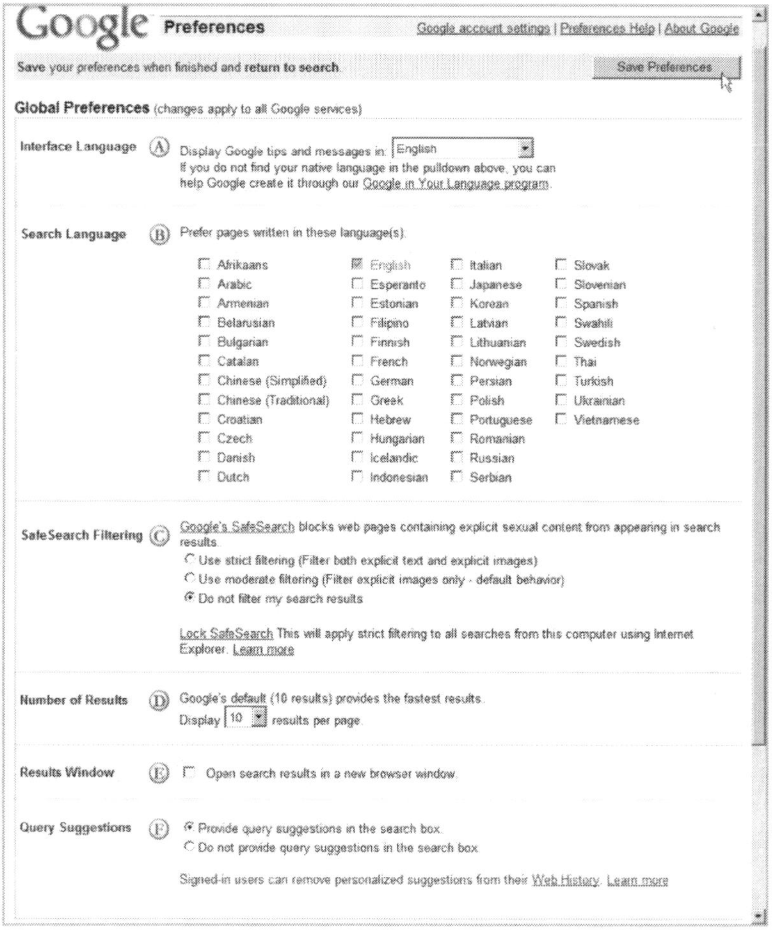

Figure A-2   The Global preferences page

Google tries to guess the location of your PC primarily from your PC's IP address. If Google can locate your PC's position, it as a rule loads your local Google homepage and set the interface language to the primary language in your region.

Although you may generally prefer to work with Google Web Search in your own language, there may be situations where you would like to change the interface language.

For example, I am writing this book in English (American) and obviously need to present all screen shots as they appear in the English version. For this reason, I am working on the US Google Homepage and using English as interface language.

Changing the Interface Language

The procedure below describes how you change the interface language from English to another language (in the example German).

1. On the US Google Homepage, click Search settings on the top of the page (Figure A-1, circled area, page 172).
2. On the Global preferences page, click on the arrow to the right of the interface language box (Figure A-3). Select the interface language you want. In the example shown in Figure A-3, German is selected as the new interface language.

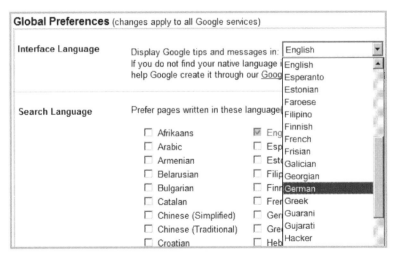

Figure A-3   Changing the interface language (here to German)

3. Click **Save Preferences** in the upper right or lower right corner of the Global preferences page (Figure A-4, circled area, page 175). To save your settings, your browser must be set to accept cookies (see page 182).

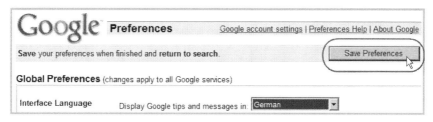

Figure A-4   Saving your global preferences

Search Language

On the next part of the Global preferences page (Figure A-2, B, page 173), you can currently (April 2010) choose between 45 additional "preferred" search languages. In addition to any preferred search language you include, Google always includes the interface language as search language (see below). You may add one or more additional search languages. Note that you can't exclude the interface language (here English) as search language. To inform you about this, English is grayed out on the form (Figure A-5).

To select an additional search language, just click in the check box to the left of the language name (Figure A-5). In the figure, I have selected German as additional search language.

Interface Language	Display Google tips and messages in: English ▾
	If you do not find your native language in the pulldown above, you can help Google create it through our <u>Google in Your Language program</u>.

Search Language	Prefer pages written in these language(s):			
	☐ Afrikaans	☑ English	☐ Italian	☐ Slovak
	☐ Arabic	☐ Esperanto	☐ Japanese	☐ Slovenian
	☐ Armenian	☐ Estonian	☐ Korean	☐ Spanish
	☐ Belarusian	☐ Filipino	☐ Latvian	☐ Swahili
	☐ Bulgarian	☐ Finnish	☐ Lithuanian	☐ Swedish
	☐ Catalan	☐ French	☐ Norwegian	☐ Thai
	☐ Chinese (Simplified)	☑ German	☐ Persian	☐ Turkish

Figure A-5   Adding a preferred search language, here German

Note that even though we have added another language, here German, as a preferred search language, English remains grayed out. This tells you that you can't prevent Google from including pages in English from the search – as long as the interface language is set to English. You get this confirmed when you make a search with these settings. In the ex-

175

ample shown in Figure A-6, I have searched for *merkel* with these settings. Google has found both English and German pages.

Figure A-6   Search results for English and German pages

Google here gives you the options to *Search the Web* or to *Search English and German pages*. Note that Google initially reports the number of
results found on the English and German pages only – although the option Search the Web has been selected automatically by Google (Figure
A-6, page 176, circled areas). When you press **Enter** or click the **Search
button**, Google correctly reports all search results (Figure A-7).

Figure A-7 Search results for the Web

When you select another interface language, for example, German, the
check box for English is not any longer grayed out. You can now leave
out English as preferred search language (Figure A-8). Note that German
is now grayed out, so you can't exclude the new interface language.

Interface Language	Display Google tips and messages in: German ▼ If you do not find your native language in the pulldown above, you can help Google create it through our Google in Your Language program.			
Search Language	Prefer pages written in these language(s):			
	☐ Afrikaans	☐ English	☐ Italian	☐ Slovak
	☐ Arabic	☐ Esperanto	☐ Japanese	☐ Slovenian
	☐ Armenian	☐ Estonian	☐ Korean	☐ Spanish
	☐ Belarusian	☐ Filipino	☐ Latvian	☐ Swahili
	☐ Bulgarian	☐ Finnish	☐ Lithuanian	☐ Swedish
	☐ Catalan	☐ French	☐ Norwegian	☐ Thai
	☐ Chinese (Simplified)	☑ German	☐ Persian	☐ Turkish

Figure A-8 Leaving out English as preferred search language

If you want to keep English as interface language, but at the same time to use another search language, you can use the Advanced Search form (see How to Select the Search Language on page 114). When you select another search language on the Advanced Search form, you still have English as interface language. Furthermore, the search results are restricted to the search language you select - here German. Figure A-9 shows the result I got when I restricted the search language to German (for the query *merkel*) on the Advanced Search form (page 114).

Figure A-9   Search results for German pages

Note how the number of search results decreased from 11,400,000 to 5,270,000, when the search was restricted to German pages. At the same time, the number of pages about the Chancellor of Germany, Angela Merkel, increased among the top 20 results (see below).

> **Google's April fool 2010**
> The screenshots in Figure A-9 and Figure A-10 were taken at the very last revision of the book on April 1, 2010. Note the unusual time units on the Statistics Bar - 0.22 microweek and 4.88e-15 epochs. I got a lot of strange time units that day! Google is well known for April fool jokes.

Finally, when we use Translated search, we get 5,190,000 German pages (Figure A-10).

Figure A-10   Translated search for the query merkel

The first 20 results achieved by using the Advanced Search form and Translated search didn't differ much. In both cases, you get about 12 (out of 20) results relating to the German Chancellor Angela Merkel. In comparison, when you just add German as a preferred search language on the Global preferences page, you only get eight results related to Angela Merkel. So, if you were looking for information about Angela Merkel, you would have got more relevant results by using either the Advanced Search form or the Translated search tool.

There is, however, an important difference between using the Advanced Search form and the Translated search tool. When you set the search language to German on the Advanced Search form, most of the results are in German. When you use Translated search, all results are in English.

If you want to find information in another language than English, your best option is generally to use Translated search. By using Translated search, you can restrict your search to another language than English without changing the interface language. It is a simple and effective way to search for results in another language - and you get the results back in English.

The example above where the query was *merkel* is very simple in the sense that the name is identical in most search languages. The benefit of using Translated search is even greater when your keyword is different in different languages. You can read about Translated search on page 70.

Of course, you shouldn't make such simple query as *merkel* at all. If you wanted to know more about the German Chancellor, a search for Angela Merkel would have given you much more relevant results.

However, even this very simple example shows that it may not be straightforward to select a new search language or to add an additional search language. You need to know about the three methods discussed above:

- Adding an extra search language under Global preferences
- Selecting an alternative search language on the Advanced Search form (page 114)
- Using Translated search (page 70) to find results in a foreign language

In most cases, Translated search is your best option: You may restrict your search to one foreign language, and you get the search results back in English. In contrast, if you have English as interface language, it may not help much to add an extra search language under Global preferences, because pages in English often make up the majority of pages and tend to depress results in other languages. Most likely, you will seldom need to add an additional preferred search language under Global preferences (see also the summary on page 183).

Safe Search Filtering

If you want to avoid getting Web pages with explicit sexual content, you may want to try Google's SafeSearch filtering.

Figure A-11   SafeSearch Filtering

You can choose between three levels of Safe Search Filtering (Figure A-11):

- *Strict filtering* filters both explicit text and explicit images. With this setting, Google tries to exclude all pages with sexual content.
- *Moderate filtering* filters explicit images only. This is Google's standard setting.
- *No filtering* doesn't filter out any result.

Until recently, you couldn't password protect your SafeSearch filtering settings. Any user of the computer could change the settings. To prevent this, Google has recently introduced a feature called Lock SafeSearch. To use Lock SafeSearch, you need to have a Google account and to be signed in. SafeSearch can only be locked at the level *strict filtering*.

In this book, we don't discuss Google features, which require a Google account. You can find some Google tips about online safety, in particular in relation to children's use of computer and Web surf at:

http://www.google.com/intl/en/landing/familysafety/

At this page, you'll also find a link to a page discussing the Lock Safe-Search feature.

Remember to save your SafeSearch settings by clicking **Save Preferences.**

Number of Results

Under this heading on the Global preferences page, you can select the number of results per page that Google displays on the results pages. You can choose between 10, 20, 30, 50, and 100. In Figure A-12, I am about to change the setting from 10 (the standard value) to 20.

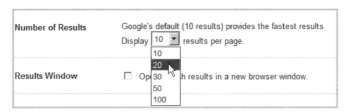

Figure A-12   Selecting number of results to be displayed per page

Ten results per windows are the standard setting. Setting a higher value allows you to skim the results faster.

Setting the Number of Results to Other Values

As mentioned on page 61, you may benefit from setting the number of results to less than the 10, when you start working with the results page so you can see its top and bottom. This way you can always see the many options Google Web Search offers for modifying your initial search. To set the number of results to be displayed to less than 10, you have to modify the URL string.

You find the URL string in your Web browser's address bar (Figure 1-1, page 5). As an example, let us assume you have searched for *google URL syntax*, and that you want Google to display five results per page.

The URL string in your browser's address bar may then look somewhat like this:

http://www.google.com/#hl=en&source=hp&q=google+url+syntax

To get Google to display five results per page, add the following at the end of the URL string:

&num=5

so the string becomes:

http://www.google.com/#hl=en&source=hp&q=google+url+syntax&num =5

Google has recently changed the URL string syntax. The URL string has become longer and more complicated to read and interpret. The actual URL string you'll get, will most likely be longer than shown in the example above. However, you can still change the number of pages displayed per page simply by adding *&num=* at the end of the string. Add the number of pages, you want displayed after the equal (=) sign. It must be a figure between 1 and 100.

There is one exception to this rule. If you have set the number of results per page on the Advanced Search form (page 112), the URL string already contains a setting for the number of pages to be displayed. If you, for example, have set the number to 30, you'll find *&num=30* somewhere in the URL string. To get another number displayed, just changed the number - for instance, from 30 to 5.

Figure A-13   Open search results in a new browser window

Results Window

The consequence of clicking the checkbox **Open search results in a new browser window** may not be obvious (Figure A-13). If you click this checkbox, Google will still present the search results page in the same window you just used for the search. However, when you click on one of the search results, Google will open the Web page in a new window. For each result you click, the matching Web page is opened in a new window. You can then easily move forth and back between different results pages. You may find this useful for comparison of a few results pages.

You shouldn't open too many windows at a time, as your screen may become cluttered.

Query Suggestions (Google Suggest)

The tool, which Google today usually calls Google Suggest, was previously called Query suggestions. On the Global preferences page, Google has kept the name Query suggestions.

Under Query suggestions, you get two options:

- Provide query suggestions in the search box
- Don't provide query suggestions in the search box

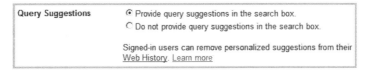

Figure A-14   Query Suggestions settings

The setting *Provide query suggestions in the search box* is the standard setting. I recommend that you keep this setting. I find the Query suggestions to be one of the most useful Google search tools. As mentioned, the Query suggestions feature is the same as Google Suggest. Google Suggest is discussed in details on page 18 to 23.

Saving Your Preferences

To be able to save your Preferences, your browser must be set to accept cookies. A cookie is a text file, which is stored on your computer to help the Web server, here the Google server, to identify your PC and your preferences. Cookies can be misused and your Web browser's Privacy Settings may, therefore, deny a Web server to store cookies on your computer.

If your browser setting doesn't allow storage of cookies, Google warns you: "Your cookies seem to be disabled. Setting preferences will not work until you enable cookies in your browser." You can read how to enable cookies (allow cookies on your computer) at:

http://www.google.com/cookies.html

Summing up

The Global preferences are your standard settings. Most likely, you are not going to change them often. Here, we briefly summarize the more important features of each setting.

The interface language is the language used for menu texts, button texts, and so on. There is seldom any need for changing the interface language.

There is a close relation between the interface language and the search language. The interface language you select under Global preferences will also be used as the primary search language by Google. Under Global preferences, you can add additional search languages, but you can't exclude the interface language. If you have English as interface language, it may not help much to add an extra search language, because pages in English often make up the majority of pages and tend to depress results in other languages.

If you want to find results in another language than the interface language, you have two better options than adding an extra search language under Global preferences.

First, you can use the Advanced Search form. It allows you to change the search language without having to change the interface language. This way, you can restrict your search to a language, which is different from the interface language. The only drawbacks are that you need to reset the search language for each browser session, and that you get many of the results in a foreign language.

Second, you can use Translated search. Here, you keep your usual interface language, you can select the search language(s) you want, and you get all results back in English. The only drawback is that you need to set up the parameters each time you want to make a Translated search.

SafeSearch filtering allows you to exclude material of explicit sexual nature. However, the protection is not very effective, because any user can change the settings back to *No filtering*. To overcome this weakness, Google has recently introduced the feature Lock SafeSearch. You can only use this feature, if you are signed in to your Google account. The Lock SafeSearch feature offers a better protection against explicit material.

You set the number of results to be displayed per page under Global preferences. The standard setting is ten. You can choose between 10, 20, 30, 50, and 100. If you want Google to display any other number, you have to modify the URL string by adding the parameter *&num=* followed by the number you want (between 1 and 100).

You may choose to have each result shown in its own window by selecting *Open search results in a new browser window*. This may be useful for comparison of a few results pages.

The last setting under Global preferences is Query Suggestions (Google Suggest). As discussed several times in the book, Query Suggestions are in general highly valuable. I suggest you keep the standard setting *Provide query suggestions in the search box*.

Closing

You have now learned all you need to know to master Google Web Search. Before we end, let us very briefly review the most important practices for effective information search on the Web.

- Use keywords that describe your topic or information need as completely and precisely as possible.
- Write keyword rich queries with at least three to four key-words - if possible more.
- Write your queries in natural language. Use short meaning-ful phrases from everyday English when you search for in-formation about common issues. Use technical language, when you search for information about technical issues.
- Use quotation marks to search for an exact phrase when needed. Don't use more than two exact phrases in one query.
- Let Google Suggest inspire and guide you to write effective queries, but don't let it control your search.
- Learn as you go. Unless you find exactly what you need after your initial query, don't stop there, but let the first results guide you to write an even better query.
- Use the Options panel to filter or expand your search as needed.
- Use Translated search to search in several languages at the same time.
- Use Translated search to search for information in a foreign language instead of adding a preferred search language un-der Global preferences.
- Use the plus operator (+) operator to enforce Google to search for specific word forms, specific spellings, and poten-tial stopwords.
- Use the minus operator (-) to filter out unwanted words, words forms, and spellings.
- Use the minus operator (-) to "subtract" or filter out a sub-group of unwanted search results.

- Use the plus operator (+) and minus operator (-) operators together to make very specific searches.
- Restrict your search to file types, sites, time period, and so on, to narrow down your search.
- Use the Advanced Search form for complex searches. It is a great assistance to write complex queries without any risk of making invalid combination of operators.
- Use the simple and complex operators directly from the search box, when you need maximum flexibility. It is highly effective, but also carries a certain risk of making invalid combinations of operators and for using operators incorrectly.
- Combine different search practices (keyword rich queries, search for meaningful phrases, filters, operators, and so on) in the same query to focus your search and to push relevant results to the top of the results list.
- Use the Options panel to do the final clean-up of your search results.

The best thing you can do from this point on is to practice the techniques you have learned in the book in your daily search for information. This way, you'll learn which features and tools to apply in different situations, and you'll learn, what works best for you. We are all different - also when we search - and what works well for one person may not suit another. Only you can find out, which techniques and tools are best for you and your search tasks. When you have found your preferred search techniques and tools, keep practicing these techniques and tools.

Besides this, you should keep an eye on how Google Web Search develops. In the 15 months, it took me to write the book, Google Web Search developed much. Among other things, new features (such as the Options panel) were added, others were improved, and the user interface changed frequently.

To help you stay current, I am preparing a Web site www.YourWeb SearchGuide.com

I plan to launch the Web site May 1, 2010 at latest. On the Web site, you'll find any updates to the book, important news about Google Web Search, and - over time - other interesting and valuable stuff about Web search. Please visit the Web site regularly!

Index

Made in the USA
Lexington, KY
03 March 2011